ULTIMATE

Surfing Adventures

100 Extraordinary Experiences in the Waves

Alf Alderson

This edition first published 2011
© 2011 John Wiley & Sons Ltd

REGISTERED OFFICE

John Wiley & Sons Ltd, The Atrium, Southern Gate, Chichester, West Sussex, PO19 8SQ, United Kingdom

EDITORIAL OFFICE

John Wiley & Sons Ltd, The Atrium, Southern Gate, Chichester, West Sussex, PO19 8SQ, United Kingdom

For details of our global editorial offices, for customer services and for information about how to apply for permission to reuse the copyright material in this book please see our website at www.wiley.com/wiley-blackwell.

The right of the author to be identified as the author of this work has been asserted in accordance

Milton Keynes Council		
2995900		
Askews		Nov-2010
797.32 ALD		£20.00

Library of Congress Cataloging-in-Publication Data
Alderson, Alf.
Ultimate surfing adventures : 100 extraordinary experiences in the waves / Alf Alderson.
p. cm.
ISBN 978-0-470-71083-8 (pbk.)
1. Surfing--Handbooks, manuals, etc. I. Title.
GV840.S8A398 2010
797.3'2--dc22
2010020779

A catalogue record for this book is available from the British Library.

Graphic Design by Holly Ramsay
Set in 8/11 TFForeverTwo
Printed in China by Toppan Leefung Printing Ltd.

Cover image: Haleiwa, Oahu, Hawai'i. Getty Images.

WILEY ✦ NAUTICAL

Wiley Nautical – sharing your passion.

At Wiley Nautical we're passionate about anything that happens in, on or around the water.
Wiley Nautical used to be called Fernhurst Books and was founded by a national and European sailing champion.
Our authors are the leading names in their fields with Olympic gold medals around their necks and thousands
of sea miles in their wake. Wiley Nautical is still run by people with a love of sailing, motorboating, surfing, diving,
kitesurfing, canal boating and all things aquatic.

Visit us online at www.wileynautical.com for offers, videos, podcasts and more.

Introduction

What is the 'ultimate surfing adventure'? Well, that depends on who you are as a surfer. Non surfers might assume it's riding the biggest, meanest, gnarliest wave on the planet, or a wave that booms ashore onto a palm-fringed beach and is surfed in boardshorts. Yet, as any surfer knows, not everyone wants to surf waves that could maim them and not everyone yearns for warm seas and the smell of sunscreen every time they paddle out.

There are plenty of people for whom surf heaven is a head high Irish reef break or a mellow Victorian beach break, even if it does mean they have to wear a wetsuit.

So what you'll find in the pages of this book is a selection of waves to appeal to everyone, from those who would ride giants to those who would ride rivers and lakes.

Hopefully a few will inspire you; maybe a few will surprise you. Perhaps a few will have you booking your next surf trip − whatever kind of surfer you are.

Alf Alderson

Dedication

To Claire

Tropical Waters

6

Temperate Waters

130

🌊 Cold Waters

184

140

South
China
Sea

Malaysia

Mentawai
Islands   Indonesia

Jakarta

Indian Ocean

Difficulty
Good intermediate –
expert

Hazards
Heavy waves and long
hold downs; shallow
reefs; sharp coral and
rocks; hot, humid climate;
malaria; infected reef cuts

Season
Year round, although
March – November
biggest and most
consistent

Water temperature
27–29°C (80–84°F)

Wetsuit
Boardshorts and rash vest;
boots useful for protection
against reefs

Access
Easy if on surf yacht
charter; surf camps will
ferry you out to the
breaks

Other local breaks
Equally world class waves
are to be found at Nias to
the north

While you're there
Take in the local culture,
which has seen relatively
little Western influence

MENTAWAI ISLANDS, INDONESIA

Disneyland for surfers

Had this book been written a decade or so ago, you'd be reading about the
Mentawais as a last frontier of surfing, where waves that no one but experts could tame
were only accessible via expensive yacht charters, where wipeouts could lead to hideous
reef cuts that sometimes turned even more hideously septic in the stifling tropical climate
and where the trade off for some of the finest barrels on Earth could well be malaria or
a broken board.

Not all of that has changed. The waves are still jade green marvels of nature that
provide some of the finest surfing in the world, the reefs are no less shallow or sharp and
those pesky mosquitoes haven't disappeared, but a surf trip to the Mentawais need no
longer be excessively difficult, excessively costly or excessively dangerous.

For sure, you can book a yacht charter and cruise in style between the breaks, but
you can also stay in a plush surf camp with all mod cons, located in front of a scintillating
selection of waves to suit pretty much every level of surfer. (Even beginners are encouraged to visit, although with no beach breaks to speak of this may be pushing it a bit.)

Many purists, of course, are spitting feathers at this desecration of one of the Holy Grails of surfing, but should perfect waves only be available to those with a deep pocket and a carving bottom turn? Who knows...

Either way, for most surfers with a reasonable level of competence or better, the Metawais are right up there as one of the places to visit. Famed breaks such as Lance's Left and Macaronis see hot surfers from all over the world parked up in their boats, ripping the exceedingly rippable walls and tucking into the aquamarine barrels that characterise both breaks.

Competition for the waves can be as hot as the climate, but there are endless other surf options along the western side of this chain of beautiful islands off the coast of West Sumatra.

Their location means that, year round, the Mentawais pick up incredibly consistent swells emanating from the southern Indian Ocean, swells so powerful that they often wrap almost right around the islands. Thus, virtually any wind direction can be offshore somewhere, although much of the time there isn't actually any wind to speak of, so you just have ideal calm, glassy conditions. It's a bit like God decided to create a Disneyland for surfers – and here it is.

The climate isn't to everyone's liking, being classically equatorial (i.e. steaming hot and often pouring with rain), but that gives you even more reason to get out into the waves as here at least you can forget about the worst of the heat.

If only every surf destination's biggest inconvenience was being too warm, hey?

South China Sea

Malaysia

Indonesia

Western Java

Indian Ocean

Australia

Difficulty
Good intermediate –
expert

Hazards
Heavy waves and long
hold downs; shallow
reefs; sharp coral, rocks
and urchins; hot, humid
climate; malaria; infected
reef cuts; some localism

Season
Year round, although April
– October is biggest and
most consistent

Water temperature
27–29°C (80–84°F)

Wetsuit
Boardshorts and rash vest;
boots useful for protection
against reefs

Access
Some of the beaches can
be easily accessed on
public transport but One
Palm is a long journey
from Jakarta involving
a boat trip; signing up
with a local surf camp
can make it considerably
easier.

Other local breaks
Try Sumatra for more
world class reef breaks

While you're there
Panaitan Island is within
the Ujung Kulon Nature
Reserve, a national park
established almost a
century ago, where Javan
rhinoceros, panthers and
tigers are among the
residents

ONE PALM POINT, WESTERN JAVA, INDONESIA

A wave to remember off the coast of Java

Several years ago, One Palm Point made its appearance in Surfer magazine after having previously gained some minor coverage in the same magazine's 'Surf Report', a low key but hardcore publication detailing surf breaks around the world.

You'd have been hard put to conjure up an image that better epitomized the drama and adventure of surf travel and discovery in those heady days before internet surf reports, email and camera phones enabled every break ever surfed to find itself online and in your living room within an hour of someone riding it.

As the name suggests, One Palm Point was defined by a solitary palm tree bowing down in front of the speeding bullet of a wave to which it bestowed its name. (Strangely, the palm rarely appears in pictures these days. Maybe it's been blown down or washed away by storms or tsunamis.)

The eponymous left hurtles shorewards across an alarmingly shallow reef on the southern tip of Panaitan Island off the coast of West Java, and it must have taken some cojones to surf it for the first time, since the take off is steep and often involves a moment or two of free fall on take off from which you have to recover instantaneously in order to get as high as possible on the face and race the lip.

Once involved in that race you don't want to go too fast, as the barrels here can hold you in their embrace for several seconds at a time; but you don't want to go too slow either, as in that case they'll hold you very tightly in that embrace before flinging you down onto the reef like so much flotsam.

The wave can be surfed when it's small and theoretically less challenging, although this means, of course, that it will be breaking in shallow water so the consequences of a wipeout in terms of hitting the reef are worse.

So, there you have it – One Palm Point, challenging but perfect when it's on, but probably not for everyone. That needn't be an issue, though, since Panaitan Island has a handful of less intimidating rights and lefts inside of One Palm Point, whilst the coast of West Java, which lies immediately east of the island, also has a fine selection of waves.

These range from heavy reefs to the easy beach breaks of Baya Beach, which are great if you're looking for a relaxed, fun session, although note that they can get busy (particularly with locals from Jakarta who can be pretty boisterous) and are at least a day's journey from Panaitan.

Given its proximity to the international air travel hub of Jakarta, the coast of West Java makes for a relatively easy introduction to Indonesian surfing, with One Palm Point being a good option to work up to – if you dare...

Difficulty
Good intermediate –
expert

Hazards
Heavy waves; shallow
reefs; sharp coral, rocks
and urchins; malaria;
infected reef cuts; crowds

Season
Year round, although April
– October is biggest and
most consistent

Water temperature
27–29°C (80–84°F)

Wetsuit
Boardshorts and rash vest;
boots useful for protection
against reefs

Access
Some of the beaches can
be accessed on public
transport but others will
require a boat, which is
usually easily arranged;
signing up with a local
surf camp can also make
it considerably easier to
access the best breaks

Other local breaks
Try Lombok (see p12) or
Bali for more world class
reef breaks

While you're there
Other than snorkelling
on the vibrant reefs and
(lots of) reading, there
isn't a great deal to do in
down time

SUMBAWA, INDONESIA

Head east for yet more Indonesian magic

Sumbawa can be accessed without excessive hassle from Lombok (see p12) or
by plane from Bali. (Bali was a serious contender to feature in this book, but for all the
undoubted quality of its waves it really isn't that much of an adventure to surf there any
longer, travelling as you are on a very well worn and busy path.)

That's not to say that Sumbawa is off the beaten track, but to travel here gives you a
slightly different take on Indonesia since it's less 'jungly' than other parts of the country
and the heat is slightly less intense. And, as with so much of the rest of Indo, you won't go
short on world beating waves.

Pioneered over 30 years ago by US and Aussie surfers, there are now plenty of locals
as well as visitors competing for Sumbawa's waves. Surfers these days hit the west coast
waves from both the shore and from surf boats, taking on some pretty serious challenges
such as the appropriately named Scar Reef and Super Suck, both fast, hollow lefts which
require speed and daring to master.

Easy, fun breaks are noticeable by their relative absence, and that doesn't change much as you head further into Sumbawa. The south coast has yet more reefs open to Roaring Forties swells that, by the time they get here, are as clean and lined up as if manufactured by machine. Two of them, Periscopes and Lakey Peak, are yet more proof that Indonesia possibly has a greater concentration of world class waves than anywhere else on Earth.

Periscopes is a very fine right that is well worth the 40-minute walk to get to and is a little less intimidating than many other breaks on Sumbawa, so it's always pretty busy. The legendary Lakey Peak just to the south is invariably prone to crowds and has a very international flavour, probably because it's an intense right and left hand peak that more than one surfer has described as the best wave they've ever ridden.

Bear in mind when surfing Sumbawa that tides can have a big influence on the quality of the waves, with some reefs being pretty much out of bounds on low tide since they're too shallow. And although the island's waves are for the most part well documented and well explored, it's still not a piece of cake to access all the breaks since slow jungle roads and an intense rainy season (November to April) can make travel difficult.

But if such things add to the sense of adventure when surfing, well, maybe that's all for the good; it makes the journey more memorable and the pay off of world class warm water waves all the more appreciated.

South
China
Sea

Malaysia

Indonesia

Lombok

Indian Ocean

Australia

Difficulty
Expert

Hazards
Heavy waves; shallow
coral reefs; rocks and
urchins; malaria; infected
reef cuts; crowds; sharks
(but no recorded attacks)

Season
Year round, although June
– September optimum for
surf and weather

Water temperature
27–29°C (80–84°F)

Wetsuit
Boardshorts and rash vest;
boots useful for protection
against reefs

Access
Good

Other local breaks
Try Bali for more world
class breaks

While you're there
If you're feeling energetic,
take a hike up the 12,224
ft Mount Rinjani, an active
volcano and Indonesia's
second highest mountain

DESERT POINT, LOMBOK, INDONESIA

A wave worth waiting for

When you observe Desert Point reeling flawlessly across the shallow coral reef
beneath its translucent blue face, you don't even need to surf it to realise that this is one
hell of a wave that fully justifies the hackneyed old term 'world class'.

And once you've ridden this amazing left, then you're hooked. From the jacking face
down which you virtually free fall, you'll grind out a gut wrenching bottom turn and then
desperately attempt to stay ahead of the foam ball trundling at high speed after the tail of
your board.

Barrel rides are the order of the day – it's almost impossible not to get shacked when
Desert Point is on – and expert surfers have been tubed here for 10, even 20 seconds
at a time. The wave just seems to go on forever, although it's so intense you'll be hard
pushed to say whether you were on it for seconds or minutes since it's such an 'in the
moment' experience.

Even better, the wave is at its best during Lombok's dry season, when the stifling humidity and intense heat for which this part of the world is known are at their least enervating, with clear blue skies coinciding with long lasting, long-period southern hemisphere ground swells spilling out their life on the southern shores of the island.

So, that's the good news. The bad news is that Desert Point isn't really as consistent as one would like. Those dry season swells need to be plenty solid and powerful to really do their stuff and it's quite possible to spend long, frustrating periods waiting for the wave to really show its class.

In fact, Lombok as a whole is not really as good or consistent as nearby Bali to the west, which, although invariably crowded, may make a better base for your surf trip. Keep an eye on the charts and the surf reports and make the short and relatively easy journey to Lombok when the forecast is looking good.

You will be sharing Desert Point with plenty of other surfers when you get here, of course, and the take off spot is tight, so catching the wave of your choice is unlikely to be a cinch. Indeed, for less experienced surfers it can all be a bit intimidating, but not to worry, there are plenty of other good waves on a decent swell. Try Grupuk Bay on the south coast, for instance; not only does it have a couple of less demanding, fun waves, the drive along the coast road is beautiful and may also reveal a few other wave riding options too.

But for those who have the skills to take it on, Desert Point is an unforgettable wave when it's firing and well worth waiting for.

Philippines
Siargao
Malaysia
Indonesia

Indian Ocean

Difficulty
Intermediate – expert

Hazards
Shallow reefs; sharp coral
and rocks; hot, humid
climate

Season
August – December

Water temperature
23–25°C (73–77°F)

Wetsuit
Shortie on cooler winter
days; boardshorts and
rash vest in summer;
boots useful for reefs

Access
Varies from easy to
long walks or boat trips
to reach the break of
your choice

Other local breaks
Good waves can be
found on the islands of
Daco, Janaza, Mamon,
Antokon and Anajauan to
the south

While you're there
Check out the natural
attractions, such as hot
springs at Lake Mainit
or the whirlpools of the
Siargao Straits

SIARGAO, PHILIPPINES

Surfing on Cloud Nine in the Philippines

Even if you haven't heard of Siargao Island, you'll know of its most famous wave,
Cloud Nine. Over the last couple of decades, this world class right has featured in
numerous magazines and videos as it barrels flawlessly across its attendant reef.

This alone would be enough to tempt many to make the somewhat arduous journey
to this south-eastern enclave of the Philippines, but there are plenty of other waves here
too, all of them reef breaks and all of them located on the eastern shores of this vaguely
fin shaped island.

In addition, the smaller islets to the south also produce good surf for those wanting to
ride waves in more isolated conditions, while easily accessible boat trips will also take you
to a handful of virtually empty world class breaks within a couple of hours.

Indeed, Cloud Nine can be very busy in prime season; what was once an exotic and
relatively isolated break that required an hour's walk from the town of General Luna
now boasts a surf camp with all the luxuries of comfortable beds, running water, toilets
and air con.

'Perfection' is the word that is often associated with Siargao's waves – clean, warm and predictable, and rarely so big that the average surfer can't enjoy them – but the island, like the rest of the Philippines, doesn't have the same consistency as other exotic tropical locations such as Indonesia and Réunion, so you have to time your visit well to make the most of the surf.

This means hitting Siargao from late summer through to early winter, when the typhoons that generate the Philippines' swell are doing their stuff to the east. The rest of the year you may score a few waves but you'll need to be lucky and they'll probably be small.

Of course, for surfers living in the northern hemisphere, heading to the tropics as winter descends is no bad thing. And if you catch Cloud Nine or its neighbours (like Tuason Point, a powerful left; Pilar, a long and forgiving right that can obtain some decent size; or Stimpy's, a fast, shallow left that's expert only territory), well, then the journey is more than worthwhile.

There's not much for novice surfers on Siargao, though; sharp coral and rocks, shallow waters and fast breaking waves are not the place to be honing the basics. But Jacking Horse, a right hander close to Cloud Nine, may be worth a look on smaller swells.

The Philippines may not be quite as exotic as they once were, now that surfing has become a mainstream activity here, but there's no doubt that a trip to Siargao when the place is firing will find you on your own personal cloud nine.

Philippine Sea

Papua New Guinea

Indonesia

Australia

Difficulty
Intermediate – expert

Hazards
Shallow reefs; sharp coral;
malaria; infected reef
cuts; sharks, stonefish,
sea snakes; some hassles
possible in busier urban
areas

Season
November – April

Water temperature
27–29°C (80–84°F)

Wetsuit
Boardshorts and rash vest;
boots useful for protection
against reefs

Access
Good to most main breaks
but a boat is essential to
optimize a trip here

Other local breaks
The hundreds of islands
and islets off Papua New
Guinea's north-east coast
are a veritable treasure
trove of breaks waiting to
be discovered

While you're there
Great snorkelling and
fishing is to be had; or
check out some of the
fascinating local
customs, which include
'shark calling'

PAPUA NEW GUINEA

Explorers welcome at one of surfing's last frontiers

In this ever shrinking world, surfers should give thanks for places like Papua New Guinea, where the combination of warm water, spectacular landscapes, exotic cultures, beautiful waves and the chance to explore all come together in an enticing package.

Two areas of this truly fascinating archipelago that are reasonably well known to surfers are Kavieng on the north coast of the rather uninspiringly named New Ireland, and the coastline either side of the town of Wewak in the north-east of New Guinea Island, both of which we'll come to in a moment.

If you want to truly get off the beaten track, then a boat (ideally), a four-wheel drive or boots and a machete can take you to remote tropical coastlines that have almost certainly never seen a surfboard on their shores. At the time of writing, for instance, 'new' waves were being discovered in the Admiralty Islands.

However, located almost on the Equator as it is, PNG's intense sun, high humidity, incredibly dense jungle and impressive array of potentially deadly critters on land and in

the sea don't exactly invite casual visitors to get out and explore, so the chances are you'll be hitting the waves at breaks that were first opened up in the 1980s.

One of the great things about many of these waves for the 'average' surfer is that the area is still quiet enough that you can score uncrowded surf and get a sense of surfing relatively new wave riding territory, while the waves rarely require the kind of the full-on commitment that is needed in places like Indonesia.

Swells here emanate from northern hemisphere storms and are usually a fairly non-intimidating three to four feet, peaking perhaps at five to six feet on bigger days. Most waves break across shallow live coral reefs to create translucent crystal cylinders into which you can tuck and shelter from the intense Equatorial sun, but monster walls of water that only the best can deal with are not that common.

Indeed, the coast either side of Wewak even offers a number of beach breaks along with a good harvest of faster reefs, making it ideal territory for mixed ability groups.

Kavieng, on the other hand, is a little more serious, with shallow reefs, fast barrels and a few real nasties in the water (think sharks, stonefish and sea snakes) making this region more of an adventure.

Although you could hang out in Kavieng town and get some fine surf at the excellent right of Picaninny, you really need to charter a boat to get to the best of what's on offer.

This will allow you access to the well surfed islands and islets of Nusa, Nago and Edmago, and breaks well beyond the horizon, up towards the Equator. Who knows, if you and your skipper are adventurous enough, you may even get to name your 'own' break...

India

Bay of Bengal

**Andaman and
Nicobar Islands**

Sri Lanka

Indian Ocean

Difficulty
Intermediate – expert

Hazards
Shallow coral; remote;
authorities may be hassly
over travel permits; some
areas off limits; intense
heat; pesky insects

Season
Summer

Water temperature
26–28°C (78–82°F)

Wetsuit
Boardshorts and rash
vest; boots useful for reef
protection

Access
A boat is required to make
the most of Andaman surf

Other local breaks
The Nicobar Islands to
the south have similar
surf conditions

While you're there
World class snorkelling
and sea fishing will while
away any downtime

ANDAMAN ISLANDS
A surf trip back in time

It's a long journey to the Andaman Islands, both in distance and time. Of the 302 lush tropical islands that thrust up out of the deep turquoise waters off the Bay of Bengal, only a handful are 'civilized'. Many are officially out of bounds to travellers, being inhabited by indigenous tribes the Onge, Jarawa and Sentinelis who have traditional lifestyles and don't take kindly to visitors. (There is an unverified report that two drunken fishermen who washed ashore on a Sentineli island in 2007 were killed.)

So the message is don't wipe out and get washed ashore on a Sentineli island! Needless to say, all the best waves on the Andamans crack across live coral reefs, and those closest to the capital of Port Blair on South Andaman can actually become relatively busy at times.

Most visitors fly into Port Blair, maybe acclimatize for a day in the fascinating and faded old colonial town and then hop aboard a surf charter yacht to make the most of what the more distant shores of these sensationally beautiful and exotic islands have to offer.

Waves arrive here thanks to those old favourites the Roaring Forties, sending long

period, perfectly lined up swells onto south and south-west facing reefs and atolls year round, but particularly through the summer months.

The offshore waters plummet to depths of over 9,000 ft, so there's little to stop the swells from hitting with a pretty powerful punch, although really big conditions are not as common as they are in Indonesia to the south-east.

It's always hot and pretty humid here, of course, being only 12° north of the Equator, but the heat and humidity is tempered if you're living offshore. Book a passage on a surf yacht charter and life can be as idyllic in the Andamans as anywhere on Earth, the more so since you're almost guaranteed empty waves.

The gin clear waters and masses of Technicolor sea life make for amazing viewing, even sitting on your board, as fish and turtles flit beneath you. In downtime, snorkelling, which is as good here as anywhere in the world, has got to be a must.

A visit to the beaches and encroaching jungle of the islands you'll be anchored off is not necessarily recommended. Apart from the steaming heat and the fact that the authorities may have designated your choice of landfall as being off limits, the sand fleas bite like bastards and can leave you with irritatingly itchy and even infected bites.

But with classic, empty aquamarine barrels to be ridden just offshore, why bother with the beach? There'll be plenty of time for wandering around on terra firma at the end of your surf trip.

Difficulty
Beginner – expert

Hazards
Crowded and occasionally aggressive lineups; shallow at some breaks; travel can involve hassle, once you're off the beaten track

Season
South-west coast, December – April; south-east coast, April – November

Water temperature
26–28°C (78–82°F)

Wetsuit
Boardshorts and rash vest; boots useful on some reefs

Access
Easy access to best known breaks

Other local breaks
The other obvious destination in this part of the world is the Maldives to the south

While you're there
Visit a national park to see wild elephants, monkeys, crocodiles etc.

SRI LANKA

This tear shaped tropical island will bring a smile to your face

As an introduction to tropical reef surfing, Sri Lanka is hard to beat. Surfers from colder climates have been beating a path to this beautiful island to sample user-friendly waves, a fascinating culture and mind blowing landscapes and wildlife for at least 40 years.

This means, of course, that the well-established spots such as Hikkaduwa and Arugam Bay are resplendent with all the dubious paraphernalia that is part and parcel of many twenty-first century surf spots: hordes of travellers from all parts of the globe (many with a limited idea of how to conduct themselves in the surf), a posse of skilled locals, surf shops, fast food outlets and cheap accommodation – everything the less discerning surfer could want, in fact.

But for the more sophisticated wave rider, Sri Lanka offers much to be discovered, with quieter reef and point breaks, particularly on the south-east coast, which you'll share with just a handful of other surfers.

The winter surf zone between Hikkaduwa and Mirissa in the south-west is characterized by quite lazy swells plonking ashore on reefs which are generally deep

enough, especially at high tide, not to be too daunting for first timers. That doesn't mean that swell of double overhead may not be found here, but it's only likely to happen on a handful of occasions each winter so if this is what you're after, look elsewhere.

But if you're searching for warm, aquamarine shoulders peeling at an inviting speed towards sunny, palm fringed shores, then you're in business. Many surfers will spend the whole surf season from December to late March hanging out along this coast, picking off waves from the small but consistent swells. During the short, flat spells they can entertain themselves with everything from visits to wildlife rich national parks, cultural centres such as Kandy in the spectacular inland mountains or an international cricket match in Galle or Colombo.

Don't be too concerned about the hostilities that have plagued Sri Lanka in recent times. These are ostensibly over now, but even when bombings and the like were taking place it was rare indeed for travellers to inadvertently become involved.

The real jewel in the crown of Sri Lanka surfing, however, is the mighty right hand point break at Arugam Bay on the south-east coast. When it's firing – which will be in summer – this is a world class break and, as such, you'll be competing hard to catch the best waves.

But there are other quality breaks in the area, which can make the long, uncomfortable journey from Colombo and the sticky summer heat worth enduring. As with the Hikkaduwa region, don't necessarily be content with surfing the well-known breaks; sniff around for some local advice and venture a little off the beaten track and the island that's famed for its gem stones may just offer up a gem of a different kind.

India

Arabian
Sea

Sri Lanka

Indian Ocean

● **Maldives**

Difficulty
Solid intermediate –
expert

Hazards
Some crowded lineups;
shallow at low tide;
dehydration and intense
sun

Season
July – August

Water temperature
26–28°C (78–82°F)

Wetsuit
Boardshorts and rash vest;
reef boots can be useful

Access
Easy but expensive

Other local breaks
Plenty of options on more
distant atolls

While you're there
If you're not surfing, this
is a chance to really chill
out for once in your life

THE MALDIVES

Indian Ocean perfection, accessed from your very own surf yacht

For pure, quality, fun waves that will have everyone grinning from ear to ear, from decent intermediate surfers to world class pros, the Maldives is hard to beat. A two-week boat charter here can easily see you score 14 consecutive days in which the surf is never less than head-high and with a little effort you can find breaks that are quiet enough to enjoy with just a handful of other like minded souls.

Indeed, very few of the Maldives' breaks can be reached without a boat, and while some surfers base themselves at holiday resorts located on one of the 26 different atolls that make up this oceanic nation, booking a boat surfari is really the best way to go.

Charter boats invariably head north from the capital Malé to a string of unpronounceable atolls ('atoll' itself is a Maldivian word) from which perfect lefts and rights roll into deepwater channels. Having a boat at your beck and call means that if one break isn't working or is too crowded, you can head to another.

You won't get the waves all to yourself, however – or not often, at least. Some breaks can get pretty busy at times, with maybe 20 surfers on a peak. But since the peaks will shift a little depending on the size of each set, you can still catch plenty of waves, whether you wait out the back or pick off the smaller inside waves. And the crowds tend to fluctuate a lot as people paddle in for a meal break or just because they're tired.

As for the surf, well, picture the perfect aquamarine barrel peeling shorewards flawlessly, and you have the typical Maldivian wave experience. The water temperature is a consistent 27°C (80°F), the waves are not too heavy and the reefs are not too shallow, so for your average surfer this truly is as good as it gets. There's a fairly even distribution of lefts and rights too, so it doesn't matter whether you're natural or goofy, you'll still find what you want.

Natural footers will particularly enjoy Sultans, Ninja's and Cola's. Sultans is a world class right that is consistent and long, with a super fast, hollow inside section (and there's the slightly bizarre left of Honky's on the other side of the peak, which actually gets bigger as you ride it). Ninja's is a short, mellowish wave popular with Japanese surfers, and Cola's is a heavy, exciting wave that picks up plenty of swell.

Even when the swell becomes less than consistent you won't get bored waiting for waves to come through, since it's a veritable marine zoo out there. You'll find dolphins surfing the waves, manta rays flapping around beyond the break, parrotfish and turtles beetling about beneath your board, and the constant exotic backdrop of palm fringed atolls.

Nowhere in the Maldives is more than 10 feet above sea level, making it the world's flattest country and, of course, the country that's most under threat from global warming, so the message is really: get there now, while you still can.

India
Myanmar (Burma)
Bay of Bengal
Sri Lanka

Difficulty
Intermediate – expert

Hazards
Serious pollution (human and industrial) at some beaches; some shallow reefs and rocks; intense heat; disease; crowded transport and busy, dangerous roads; flooding, electrical storms and drought

Season
May – August

Water temperature
26–29°C (78–84°F)

Wetsuit
Boardshorts and rash vest; reef boots

Access
Breaks in towns and cities easy to access; elsewhere, four-wheel drive will be useful

Other local breaks
Sri Lanka

While you're there
Immerse yourself in the local culture and get down with the locals, some of the funnest, friendliest people you'll meet

BAY OF BENGAL, INDIA

One of the world's most crowded countries, with some of the world's least crowded waves

Considering the vastness of India's coastline and the fact that it's been on the traveller's trail for decades, it's something of a mystery as to why the country remains so unsurfed. Unless you've travelled there, that is.

Because, for all its charms and fascinations, no one would call India an easy place in which to move around. Sure, it's cheap and the railways will take you pretty much anywhere, but it has a challenging climate and it's spectacularly crowded. And when you add a surfboard and backpack to that equation, well, there are far easier coastlines to explore.

But assuming you've fought your way to the hot and sticky coastline of the Bay of Bengal, you might find some decent waves, bearing in mind that there's well over 600 miles of shoreline facing south to south-east, which is thus well in line to pick up swells from the Indian Ocean to the south, as well as south-west monsoon swells that coincide with the peak surf season.

Unfortunately, this may well coincide with predominantly onshore winds, but mornings will invariably bring clean, offshore conditions before the onshores start to pick up, so don't necessarily write it off.

And the one thing you can be absolutely sure about when you score a few good waves here is that you'll have them pretty much to yourself. User friendly right hand point breaks are a feature of the coastline either side of the area's main city of Vishakhapatnam ('Vizag'), a ridiculously busy place both in and out of the ocean (with fishing boats and other marine craft, not surfers). Vizag also has a number of beaches of varying degrees of cleanliness, which may be worth checking out.

Unfortunately, and perhaps not surprisingly, pollution can be a major issue close to industrial centres like Vizag, and it's not just from industry – many residents use the beach as a toilet, so it can be worth avoiding golden strands alongside large population centres at anything other than high tide.

Your best bet, though, is to use Vizag as a point of entry and then, like surf pioneer and photographer John Callahan (one of the few to have recorded the Bay of Bengal's surf), head north or south and explore.

A good option to the north is Mangamari, where long, long beach breaks and a quality right will encourage all levels of ability to get into the water. To the south is still very much terra incognita as far as waves are concerned although there are doubtless plenty of discoveries to be made.

Without a doubt, India's Bay of Bengal is a surf adventure in the making, and if it doesn't come up with the goods you're but a very interesting hop, skip and a jump from Sri Lanka and its guaranteed crystal cylinders.

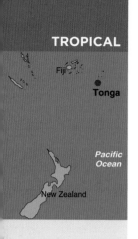

Fiji

Tonga

Pacific
Ocean

New Zealand

Difficulty
Strong intermediate –
expert

Hazards
Shallow live coral reefs

Season
Year round, but April –
August most consistent

Water temperature
22–26°C (71–78°F)

Wetsuit
Boardshorts and rash
vest; boots useful for
protection against reefs;
shortie may be useful on
cooler/breezier days

Access
Good to most breaks

Other local breaks
If you have access to a
boat there are a multitude
of options on the
offshore reefs

While you're there
Great snorkelling and
fishing are available, as
well as world class diving

TONGATAPU, TONGA
A small piece of Polynesian surf perfection

The Tonga archipelago is just one of scores of incredibly exotic South Pacific island chains fringed by shallow, live coral reefs and surrounded by deep blue ocean that in some places plummets to a depth of over 30,000 feet just a few miles offshore.

Visited by Captain Cook in the 1770s, when he named them 'The Friendly Islands' on account of the inhabitants' gentle natures, the islands are the only remaining Polynesian kingdom, with a lineage of sovereigns that goes back a thousand years.

Seas hereabouts are swept on an almost daily basis by powerful swells marching north from the lower latitudes of the Roaring Forties where storms and gales race around the globe like mad dogs, with no land to block their easterly progress and only small islands like Tongatapu to trip up the swells they generate.

Add to that balmy trade winds that hold up the faces of breaking waves and produce fast, barrelling walls as a matter of course and you have the perfect Polynesian mix of hot sun, gentle breezes, warm water and consistent surf. No wonder surfing was born in this corner of the globe.

Although only some 15 miles across at its widest point, Tongatapu is the biggest of almost 200 islands in the Tonga archipelago and it's relatively easy to get to and around.

Most of the island's breaks are concentrated in a small stretch at the north-west end, where south-west swells wrap around and grind ashore on a reef that is fanned by offshore trade winds from the east and south-east for much of the year.

All the breaks are within a few minutes' walk of each other and are but a short paddle offshore, and they don't get excessively crowded so Tongatapu really is rather inviting – up to a point.

Virtually without exception, every break on the island is shallow; and the live coral that appears as clear as day beneath the glassy wave faces is sharp and unforgiving if you bounce across it. Indeed, even though tidal ranges around Tonga are minimal, many spots are nevertheless too shallow to surf at low tide.

Perhaps the least challenging of the waves is Corners, a long left that's a little deeper than the waves either side of it and on less intense summer swells can be taken on by relative novices. But then, you don't come to Tongatapu to surf mushy little beach breaks. This is a destination for those who want to take on the challenge of fast, barrelling walls.

Indeed, you can make your trip even more memorable by taking a boat trip out to some of the breaks to the north of the island, where various reefs offer plenty of serious waves and fewer surfers taking them on. It's easy and cheap to rent a boat for the short trip, or if you stay at one of the island's surf camps they can sort it all out for you.

Coral Sea

New
Caledonia   Fiji

Brisbane

Australia

Tasman Sea

VITI LEVU, FIJI

Surf paradise – or is it?

While there's no end of superlative warm water surf in the South Pacific, Fiji is possibly more synonymous than any other archipelago with surf perfection thanks to glorious scenery, clear azure seas, amazingly consistent surf and the fact that there's never any need to wear more than boardshorts and plenty of sunscreen when surfing here.

The western side of the main island of Viti Levu is the focal point of Fijian surfing, with the two phenomenal lefts of Cloudbreak and Restaurants topping the long list of exceptional breaks in the area. Unfortunately, both waves are privately 'owned' and you can't access them unless you pay big bucks to stay at the surf camp in front of them, or, to be more precise, you can't access them without getting serious hassle if you're not staying in the surf camps, which only goes to show that, as ever, humans can always screw up paradise.

Not to worry, though, there are plenty of other superb waves to be had on Fiji and to be honest both Cloudbreak and Restaurants are the territory of expert surfers only, with the consequences of messing up here being way heavier than the local enforcers.

However, you will need to use a boat to get to the majority of the waves, such as the fast and bowly rights of Wilkes Pass or the equally challenging Namotu Lefts, and since most visitors stay at one of the island's other surf camps this will all be organized for you. (If you're travelling independently, boat hire can be arranged for fairly reasonable fees.)

And while Fiji has a bit of a hardcore reputation, you can still enjoy a surf trip here if grinding double overhead barrels are not your thing, since that rare South Pacific beast, a beach break, is to be found at Sigatoka Beach to the south of the main reef breaks, as well as a shorter and more punchy shore break at nearby Natadola Beach.

The waves at Sigatoka break off sandbanks at the mouth of the Sigatoka River, where you'll find both lefts and rights with nice long walls, although they tend to get blown out by mid-morning.

In terms of scoring waves you'd be pretty unlucky not to get in some great sessions whatever time of year you choose to visit Fiji, since its location in the Pacific is remarkably exposed to swells from all directions, particularly the south-west. For the primo swells you should be here between March and October; this has the added and very huge benefit of ensuring you miss the wet and humid weather that hits the island in the other half of the year (perhaps just to prove that even nature isn't perfect).

Difficulty
Intermediate – expert

Hazards
Sharp, shallow reefs and very heavy waves; intense sun and dehydration; proprietorial 'ownership' of some of the best waves

Season
Year round, but April – October best

Water temperature
25–28°C (77–82°F)

Wetsuit
Boardshorts and rash vest; reef boots advisable

Access
Most breaks are accessed by boat, easily arranged

Other local breaks
A boat trip to outer reefs will almost certainly turn up the goods

While you're there
There's fantastic snorkelling and diving, and the fishing is also excellent so you can easily catch your own dinner

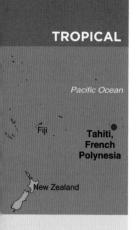

Pacific Ocean

Fiji

Tahiti,
French
Polynesia

New Zealand

Difficulty
Beginner – expert

Hazards
Sharp, shallow reefs
and unbelievably heavy
waves; intense sun and
dehydration

Season
Year round, but April –
October best

Water temperature
25–28°C (77–82°F)

Wetsuit
Boardshorts and rash
vest; reef boots advisable;
helmet worth considering
for some breaks

Access
Most reef breaks are
accessed by boat,
easily arranged

Other local breaks
A boat trip to outer reefs
will deliver yet more
world class waves

While you're there
Take a trip into Tahiti's
spectacular mountains
– not only is the scenery
amazing, it can be a
good way of escaping the
hotter days on the coast

TAHITI

Killer waves in every sense of the word

Just over a decade ago, Tahiti was just another South Pacific island group with good, consistent surf, much like so many other similar archipelagos. And then Teahupoo burst onto the scene.

We'll come to this freak of nature in a moment, but for ordinary mortals who prefer the waves they ride to be fun rather than a dance with death, Tahiti actually has quite a lot to recommend it.

Tahiti receives regular swell year round, with April to October being the peak period, and this pounds ashore on the island's stunning south and south-west facing coasts at spots such as Vairao, where lefts of perfect shape and stature crank shorewards like something out of a goofy foot's dream. Even novices can enjoy their own taste of paradise on the beach breaks at nearby Papara.

Elsewhere there are quality waves on nearby Moorea Island and in the 'off season' of November to March more than adequate north and north-west swells lay down plenty of challenge on Tahiti and Moorea's north coasts.

But it's Teahupoo that Tahiti is all about these days, a car crash of a wave that, when first seen, can barely be believed. As south-westerly swells run up against the painfully shallow reef here, it seems at times as if the entire ocean has risen up to devour the reef. Quite simply, the surface of the sea behind the wave appears to be several yards higher than the land it's about to pulverize – you don't get the kind of distinct wave form that 'normal' waves create.

When this monster left is really going off it has to be towed into in order to ensure a safe drop down the concave face of the wave, and even then there's every chance you'll free fall for part of that drop.

Assuming you make the drop – and you really want to, since having what appears to be the entire Pacific land on top of you in three feet or so of water above a live coral reef isn't a good experience – there are no fancy bottom turns, top turns or turns of any other sort involved in riding 'Chopes'. It's simply foot to the floor and scream along the muscled green face of the wave as a six-foot thick lip throws over your head and slices down several yards in front of you while a time bomb of a foam ball hunts you down from behind.

If you make it, you're an instant surf hero. If you don't, you're still a hero because you dared to take it on, although you may well be a maimed and bloodied hero and it should never be forgotten that people have died surfing here.

So you could say Tahiti really does have it all – spectacular landscapes, a lovely climate and waves that can do everything from putting a grin on your face to killing you...

Coral Sea

Fiji

New Caledonia

Australia

Tasman Sea

Difficulty
Beginner (but limited
options) – expert

Hazards
Shallow reefs and fast
heavy waves; sharks; long
exposure to intense sun
on offshore reefs

Season
May – October

Water temperature
22–27°C (71–80°F)

Wetsuit
Boardshorts and rash vest;
boots useful for reefs;
a shortie will be useful in
winter if you feel the cold

Access
Virtually all breaks are
accessed by boat

Other local breaks
A surf charter yacht will
take you to endless reef
break options

While you're there
Horse racing is something
of a national sport, so
check out a race meeting
and chance a few bucks in
the capital Nouméa

NEW CALEDONIA

New Caledonia – a long way from 'old' Caledonia in every way

Named by Captain Cook, who apparently considered that its rugged green coastline resembled that of Scotland (presumably he'd only ever been to Scotland in exceptionally good weather), New Caledonia contains an eclectic mix of French and Polynesian cultures and remains a French colony, although a referendum on independence is due in the near future.

This means that when you're out in it the region's glittering waves you're likely to hear French being spoken in the lineups, which remarkably don't tend to be that busy when you consider the world class quality of so much of the surf. Neither is localism a serious issue.

New Caledonia is made up of a main island, Grand Terre, the Loyalty Islands to the north-east and several smaller islands, and is located in the warm waters of the south-western Pacific. The surf is not as consistent as you might expect as the area is in the swell shadow of both Australia and New Zealand, which block some of the Roaring Forties swells that would otherwise pound the southern shores.

One of the best known spots is Ouano, a remarkably consistent left and a shorter right. Ouano lies several miles offshore and is visited by boats manned by both New Caledonian locals and guests of Grande Terre's various surf camps.

Depending on how the swell is hitting, Ouano can vary from a fast, barrelling face to more mellow walls and it's often a very long ride of up to 300 yards. Like virtually all the breaks in this huge archipelago you need some form of boat access to reach it, since New Caledonia's waves all break on distant offshore coral reefs where the power of the swells remains undiminished – which means this isn't the place to be if you're not a reasonably accomplished surfer.

However, there is a beach break on Terre Grande at La Roche Percée, which is far less demanding than its offshore counterparts. A long river-mouth left, it can be taken on by beginners as well as longboarders looking for a mellow session in the tropical sun.

New Caledonia is becoming an increasingly popular spot with Aussie surfers making their escape from colder winter waters, since the best and most consistent waves occur in the austral winter from May to October, when it's pretty rare to get waves smaller than head high.

And sitting out at one of the many reef breaks, sun beating on your back and turtles and manta rays gliding beneath your board as you wait for the next long distance swell to grind ashore with mechanical precision, it's kind of easy to understand what the attraction is.

Difficulty
Good intermediate –
expert

Hazards
Shallow reefs and fast
heavy waves; long
exposure to intense sun
on offshore reefs; malaria;
dodgy drinking water

Season
December – April

Water temperature
28–29°C (82–84°F)

Wetsuit
Boardshorts and rash vest;
boots useful for reefs

Access
Virtually all breaks are
accessed by boat

Other local breaks
Endless options
throughout the 17,000
square-mile archipelago

While you're there
Check out the skull
shrines on Skull Island;
and the scuba diving,
snorkelling and sea
fishing are world class

SOLOMON ISLANDS

Try and keep your head when you're surfing here

The Solomon Islands make up the third largest archipelago in the South Pacific,
with over 900 islands and islets and a vast number of surf spots, the majority of which
are yet to be ridden.

One of the best explored regions is around New Georgia Island in the west of the
archipelago, which fits everyone's idea of a South Pacific island perfectly. Dense green
forests in the interior flow down to white sand beaches, above which palm trees reach out
to impossibly blue seas, while out on the island's fringing reefs the water turns blinding
white as powerful swells explode into the shallow waters.

And there's even a wild and fascinating history to go with the islands. In days gone
past, tribal warfare involved the practice of head hunting, which apparently demonstrated
bravery and, if successful, also increased the value of a warrior's soul. The sinister
remains of the practice can still be seen at the appropriately named Skull Island, which
also happens to have one of the best right handers in the islands just a few hundred
yards offshore.

Indeed, Skull Island (the break) is as good an introduction to the Solomon Islands as you'll get. A precise and predictable right walls across a shallow reef before petering out in a deep lagoon of bathwater warm water and if you forget about the island's grisly past this is a gorgeous place to surf, albeit quite a long boat ride to access.

But then, a boat is essential to make the most of all the breaks around the New Georgia Islands. Fortunately, they can easily and inexpensively be hired from population centres such as Gizo or Munda, or you can stay in a resort such as Zipolo Habu on Lola Island, which will take you out to the breaks as well as providing you with such essentials as a soft bed and a cold beer after a tough day in the surf.

If you want to explore further afield, the Solomon's biggest island, Santa Isabel (to the north of New Georgia), is also now opening up to surf tourism. As with the rest of the archipelago there are more breaks in the area than you could ever hope to surf, however long you stay, so you can be pretty sure of getting pristine South Pacific perfection to yourself.

However, you should be aware that most land is tribally owned and you may have to get permission before being allowed to surf some spots, not so much because the owners want the surf for themselves but because you may be trespassing on fishing grounds.

And if you can't get that permission, well, don't worry too much, there are more than enough alternative surf spots.

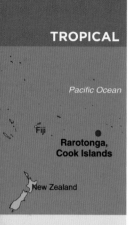

Pacific Ocean

Fiji

**Rarotonga,
Cook Islands**

New Zealand

Difficulty
Good intermediate –
expert

Hazards
Shallow reefs; intense sun

Season
April – September

Water temperature
24–27°C (75–80°F)

Wetsuit
Boardshorts and rash vest;
boots useful for reefs

Access
Virtually all breaks are
accessible by car; many
more may be found if you
have access to a boat

Other local breaks
Endless options
throughout the rest of this
immense archipelago

While you're there
Hire a moped and explore
the island; stop off en
route and hit one of the
hiking trails up into the
mountains

RAROTONGA, COOK ISLANDS

Stop over and grab a few barrels in Rarotonga

It seems only fair that Captain James Cook, the man who probably saw more world class surf in his time than anyone other than modern day surf explorers, should have some beautiful South Pacific islands named in his honour (although the locals may disagree). But it has to be said that the native names do sound better. The capital island of Rarotonga conjures up all the exotic beauty of this entrancing part of the world far better than the surname of a British explorer.

The 13 Cook Islands cover an immense area of more than a million square miles, with phenomenal exposure to swells from pretty much 360°, and it's unlikely their real surf potential will ever be fully realized. However, many places that have been explored don't quite live up to expectations, since the shape and alignment of the reefs and the underwater topography isn't ideal for moulding swells into perfect surf.

That said, for anyone used to enduring the kind of cold, grey conditions that are common to the home of their namesake Captain Cook, the waves breaking here are still very much worth checking out, particularly on Rarotonga, a small round volcanic island rising steeply out of the deep blue Pacific to a height of over 2,000 ft. It's the easiest of the Cook Islands to access, as well as being the stopping off point for flying onto other islands in the group.

Another plus point for surfing on Rarotonga is that unlike many South Pacific islands you don't need a boat to access the breaks, as many of them are but a relatively short paddle from the shore. Nevertheless, they are still pretty shallow, so much so that you'll generally want to hit the waves at high tide rather than risk hitting the live coral reefs at low tide.

The most popular spot is at Avana on the east coast, where you'll find short, shallow lefts and rights that are popular with the local body boarders, whilst the main town of Avarua also has a decent left and there are very acceptable rights at Club Raro and Norrie Park on the north and east shores respectively.

A good road skirts the coast so all these spots and others are easily accessible. Perhaps surprisingly, once you get away from Avana and Avarua crowds are rarely an issue and most travellers you encounter are likely to be on a round the world ticket rather than here for a long stay, picking off a few waves in Rarotonga en route to more popular surf destinations such as Hawai'i and New Zealand.

So, if you're doing the Round the World thing and the Cook Islands are an optional stop off, they're worthy of serious consideration. After all, relatively uncrowded tropical reef breaks aren't something you come across every day.

Western Samoa

Fiji

Pacific Ocean

Difficulty
Good intermediate –
expert

Hazards
Shallow reefs;
intense sun; sharks

Season
April – September

Water temperature
27–29°C (80–84°F)

Wetsuit
Boardshorts and rash vest;
boots useful for reefs

Access
Several breaks are
accessible by car; many
more options open up if
you have access to a boat

Other local breaks
Endless options around
the eight additional islets
in the area

While you're there
There's some superb
diving to be had, or check
out a rugby match in the
capital Apia; the Samoans
are some of the best –
and biggest – players on
the planet

SAVAI'I AND UPOLU ISLANDS, WESTERN SAMOA

Great waves and a fascinating and friendly culture

There's more surf than you can shake a stick at in the islands of Western Samoa, and most of it is of a serious nature. Fast, heavy wave faces, freight-training down shallow live coral reefs where you can't afford to muck about, and you certainly shouldn't be paddling out unless you're a very competent surfer.

Easy beach breaks are a rarity and for the hardcore surfer likely to be drawn to this part of the South Pacific they're not likely to be of any great interest, but if you want an easy introduction to surfing the islands your best bet is to head to the north shore where the waves don't generally have as much power and size as the south coast.

Savai'i is the largest island in Western Samoa, Upolu the second largest (although with the biggest population) and both attract enormous amounts of swell year round, since

they're so exposed. Waves of 20 ft or more are not uncommon on winter swells marching up from the Roaring Forties, and whilst summer is considerably smaller there's always the chance of a cyclone swell banging into the north coast of both islands (or, if you're unlucky, one may actually cross the region).

Unlike many South Pacific islands a large number of breaks are accessible from the shore so, while access to a boat will open up many more surf options, it's not vital.

Both islands have the classic South Pacific landscape of volcanic mountains rising up out of the ocean (the highest point being 6,095 ft Mauga Silisili on Savai'i), the slopes of which are festooned in dense, wet jungle and fall away steeply to lush, fertile valleys and the pristine reef fringed coastline below.

The people are renowned for being some of the friendliest in the South Pacific and they have retained strong cultural traditions, so much so that you may find that in some areas surfing on Sunday is frowned upon. On the other hand, get chatting to a local and you may well find yourself invited for a traditional Samoan meal and to meet the family.

In many ways this is part of the attraction of Western Samoa. Many South Pacific and Indian Ocean surf areas can only be accessed effectively by boat and if you're living aboard the vessel you enjoy relatively little contact with the local people and their culture. This is not the case on Savai'i or Upolu and whilst the surf is so consistent, especially in winter, that you can surf pretty much every day, it's well worth taking time out of the water to experience the islands themselves as well as the fantastic waves that surround them.

TROPICAL

Pacific Ocean

● **Micronesia**

Papua New Guinea

Coral Sea

Australia

Difficulty
Expert

Hazards
Shallow reefs and fast heavy waves; sharks, barracuda and stonefish; strong rips; remote

Season
December – April

Water temperature
28–29°C (82–84°F)

Wetsuit
Boardshorts and rash vest; boots for reefs

Access
Most breaks can only be accessed by boat

Other local breaks
Thousands, if you have a boat to explore

While you're there
Pohnpei and Kosrae are quite mountainous so hiking is a good option, especially to the numerous waterfalls and viewpoints such as that from the top of Sokehs Rock on Pohnpei – but take good rain gear

MICRONESIA

Small islands, perfect waves and never likely to be surfed out

Micronesia consists of literally thousands of idyllic looking islands, islets and atolls spread across a staggering 2.4 million square miles of the western Pacific to the east of the Philippines and Indonesia (the name derives from the Greek for 'small island').

This tropical location means that the spectacularly clear turquoise waters that surround the islands are not just amongst the warmest in the world but are also open to plentiful swell from all directions, and the opportunities for surf exploration here are legion. There are literally thousands of breaks to be discovered by anyone who has a yacht and it's a fair bet that many of these may never be surfed.

Three of the region's larger islands give you a good idea what to expect if you surf here: Yap, the westernmost island in Micronesia; Kosrae, one of the most beautiful islands, with an uninhabited mountainous interior and some 8,000 residents living on the shores of its 15 square miles; and Pohnpei, the largest island and one of the wettest places on Earth with up to 400 inches of rain a year in the mountainous interior.

The reefs that fringe each of these islands produce a magnificent array of the kind of empty, photogenic translucent barrels that surf dreams are made of, but you need to have your wits about you when surfing most breaks since they're fast, heavy and shallow.

The best known spot in the region is Palikir Pass, or 'P-Pass' on Pohnpei. This fickle but world class right has appeared on the cover of many a surf mag since it was first revealed to the outside world in a 1998 copy of Surfer magazine's 'Surf Report', which described it as "a bowly right, which is the most consistent wave on the island". Nothing much has changed since, other than it will now have considerably more surfers on it than when the lucky Surf Report guys were here, as there's now a surf camp on Pohnpei.

For all their undoubted beauty and 'come hither' looks, the brilliant waves of Micronesia are not a place for anyone other than very competent surfers. There are no easy beach breaks to speak of, since all the islands here are surrounded by fringing reefs on which break the multifarious swells that roll across this part of the Pacific. While some are less challenging than others (such as Lelu and Tafunsak on Kosrae, and Main Channel on Yap), their shallow nature means that you've got to keep wipeouts to a minimum.

And perfect conditions are not absolutely guaranteed. It is possible to get day after day of blown out conditions and rain. But Micronesia's relative inaccessibility and the challenging nature of the surf mean that there are, and always will be, countless perfect gin clear warm water breaks out there.

Coral Sea

Queensland

Australia · Brisbane

New South Wales

Sydney · Tasman Sea

Difficulty
Beginner – expert

Hazards
Aggressive lineups;
sharks; fast, heavy
waves; rocks/shallow at
some breaks

Season
Year round

Water temperature
18–26°C (64–78°F)

Wetsuit
3/2 steamer in winter
through to boardshorts in
summer

Access
Easy access to virtually all
breaks but parking may
be a problem at some

Other local breaks
More great point breaks to
the north on the Sunshine
Coast; quieter breaks
further south into NSW

While you're there
Head inland to visit the
lush rainforests and
mountains

NORTHERN NEW SOUTH WALES/ SOUTHERN QUEENSLAND

Right on

The strip of coastline either side of the Queensland/NSW border is without doubt amongst the most welcoming a surfer could ever hope to find. Well – it was in the '60s and '70s when its wave riding potential was being uncovered by the likes of Nat Young, the former world surfing champion, who still lives in the area.

Imagine stumbling across mile after mile of golden beaches, verdant headlands and hidden coves backed by wild, lush rain forest and fronted by sapphire blue seas onto which warm water swells break pretty much year round. Little wonder that Surfer's Paradise was so named (even though it has nowhere near the best surf in the region).

Today, of course, everyone wants a piece of this once idyllic action and, while breaks like Kirra and Angourie are ideal spots to watch some of the highest performance surfing on Earth, they're not easy places to score wave after wave unless your name is Mick Fanning or Joel Parkinson (two more local latter day world champs).

But even the competition in the water and the urban sprawl on land is not enough to stop thousands of surf pilgrims giving it a go here every year. You could justifiably argue that if you can hack it here you can hack it anywhere, so for you young guns out there who think you're hot shots, this is the place to come and see if you measure up...

Beach breaks such as hectic Duranbah ('D-bah') have fun peaks pretty much year round. If you want a more mellow scene, head south to hippy-dippy Byron Bay where you can get a work out in the water then relax in all manner of exotic, esoteric ways from massage to aromatherapy, or just with a cold beer.

But it's the right hand point breaks that you really come here for. The aforementioned Kirra and Angourie along with other classics like Burleigh, Superbanks and Lennox Heads all offer world class crystalline walls that sparkle an invite that's impossible to resist.

All are renowned worldwide for their speed, power, hollowness and all round perfection, and one good session at any of these spots will have you addicted. It could well be the one time in your life you wish you were about 70 years old, since that would have given you the chance to be here as a young shaver when these breaks were first being ridden and all was love, peace and general grooviness in the water.

One can but imagine what those halcyon days were like but even today, with crowds, traffic and twenty-first century madness all part and parcel of surfing the area, it has to be worth a visit. Just one good wave at Kirra or Lennox will convince you of that.

China

East China
Sea

●Taiwan

Hong Kong

South China
Sea

Difficulty
Beginner – expert

Hazards
Some breaks can get
busy; typhoons may
be a hazard if they
track across the island

Season
Year round but
late summer/early
autumn best

Water temperature
22–28°C (71–82°F)

Wetsuit
Boardshorts and
rash vest in summer,
shortie in winter

Access
Good to all of the
popular breaks

Other local breaks
Closest major surf
destinations are The
Philippines and Japan

While you're there
Bring a camera and
explore the fascinating
landscapes and culture
of the island once
called 'Ilha Formosa'
('Beautiful Island') by
Portuguese explorers

TAIWAN

Typhoons bring late summer action to Taiwan's coasts

Tucked in between China's south-east coast and the north coast of the Philippines, Taiwan is a surf destination with a difference. Like so much of modern day Asia, it's a fascinating mix of the ultra modern and the ancient when you're on land, and out in the surf you can encounter remarkably good waves if you catch it at the right time.

When the 'right time' occurs is a matter of opinion. Like most places, winter sees a lot of swell action, but this is also the coldest time of year, of course, when air and water temperatures can dip low enough to make some form of neoprene useful.

In summer, both air and water warm up dramatically, with both getting into the mid to high 20s Celsius (70s–80s Fahrenheit), along with typically tropical humidity, and typhoon swells as summer pushes into autumn.

Taiwan's east coast also has reasonably consistent small summer swells courtesy of the large fetch of the western Pacific, so a late summer/early autumn visit may see you scoring the best combination of weather and fun summer surf along with a few stonking typhoon swells.

That's not to say the west coast doesn't get waves too. There's an active longboard scene, for instance, on Penghu Island off Taiwan's west coast, where the waves tend to be

smaller and less powerful than on the east coast (hence the longboards), although it can pick up some good southerly swells.

Taiwan is a leaf shaped island around 245 miles long by 89 miles wide, with a coastline of 973 miles. It has good transport and access to most breaks, so it's not too hard in a week or so to search out all the best spots along the east coast from north to south. About 25 miles to the west, the Penghu group has a total area of 79 square miles.

The focal point of activity in the north is Dashi, or Honeymoon Bay, where the south swells of summer and the north-easterly swells of winter provide waves year round in the form of some reasonable beach breaks and a long right at the south end of the bay. However, being close to the busy city of Taipei, you can expect them to be crowded when they're on.

Down at the south end of the country the island tapers away into a long and gradually narrowing peninsula where swells roll ashore on both the west and east coasts and there's a good chance of offshore winds somewhere, thanks to the varying angles of the coastline.

There's a varied range of beach breaks, cobblestone rivermouths and reefs here, which provide surf for all levels of ability, and they're pretty consistent, not too crowded and the locals are friendly, making it well worth the trek from the north.

In fact it's worth getting here sooner rather than later, since Taiwan is now marketing itself quite aggressively as a tourist destination, which, if the rest of the world is anything to go by, probably means it's only a matter of time before the island's fine array of surf breaks become busier than one might like.

Mongolia   Japan

Beijing

China
•

Hong Kong

*South
China
Sea*

Difficulty
Beginner – expert

Hazards
Pollution; crowds in HK;
typhoons may be
a hazard if they track
across the region

Season
Year round, but late
summer/autumn best

Water temperature
Hong Kong:
20–28°C (68–82°F)
Hainan:
24–29°C (75–84°F)

Wetsuit
Boardshorts and rash
vest in summer, shortie
in winter; possibly 3/2
steamer in Hong Kong

Access
Good to the better
known breaks

Other local breaks
Taiwan is the closest
place with a developed
surf scene

While you're there
In Hong Kong, the city
will keep you plenty
occupied if it's flat; in
Hainan, spend some time
exploring the country, its
lovely landscapes and its
Buddhist culture

CHINA

The slumbering giant of surfing starts to wake

Relative to its landmass, China has a comparatively short coastline that is only
a little longer than the UK's, but you're still likely to have any waves that roll onto that
coastline to yourself, for surfing has yet to take off here.

When it does, well, let's just say the big guns of the surf world are ready and waiting
to make the most of the planet's biggest untapped market. (There are already a dozen
Quiksilver stores in the country, for instance, many of them about as far from the ocean
as you can get).

As far as wave riding is concerned, Hong Kong is the focal point. Expats have surfed
the waves here since the '60s, and there's now a healthy local surf population. The hub
of the action is Big Wave Bay HK, which doesn't necessarily live up to its name and can
get pretty crowded on a good swell, and Tai Long Wan SK, which is a better bet since the
waves tend to have more shape here and the water is cleaner.

There are several other very surfable point breaks along the coast to the north-east
of Hong Kong. Don't be fooled into thinking you'll find the kind of crowds here that are
normally associated with the city – it can actually be rather quiet and peaceful once you
escape the urban throng.

Winter is the most consistent season, with swells emanating from the north-east monsoon, although bigger and more exciting waves can show up in summer when the typhoon season is in full swing.

Just down the coast from Hong Kong (although bear in mind that this is China so 'just down the coast' means 300 miles away) is Hainan Island, more traditionally 'Chinese' than Hong Kong and the spot where the country's home grown surf scene is slowly taking off.

Open to the same swells as Hong Kong, the island's burgeoning surf scene is being encouraged by a small expat owned surf school, along with occasional visits from overseas surfers, particularly the Japanese, who are looking to enjoy the quality left hand points that are a feature of the island's south-east coast.

Locals here who are keen to get into surfing face various cultural hurdles that are pretty much unique to China. For a start, the country tends to encourage conformity amongst its 1.3 billion residents, whereas surfing is surely one of the most non-conformist sports out there.

Then there's the fact that surfing gives you a healthy tan; not good in China, where a tan is looked upon as a sign that you're a member of the peasantry!

There are also some serious cases of water pollution to deal with. The environment isn't China's primary concern as it surges onward to become the world's number one industrial power.

But then, no native Indonesians surfed 40 years ago and look at the number of locals ripping it up in the waves of Indo today. So it can only be a matter of time before Chinese waves are awash with surfers. Best get there now, before it gets crowded out.

Dubai

Saudi
Arabia

Oman

Yemen

Arabian
Sea

Difficulty
Beginner – expert

Hazards
Intense heat and
dehydration; some
rocky reefs; potential
culture clashes; harsh
travelling conditions

Season
Winter for United Arab
Emirates' north coast;
summer for Oman's
south coast

Water temperature
20–30+°C (68–86+ °F)

Wetsuit
Boardshorts and rash vest;
boots useful for protection
against reefs

Access
Good to main breaks
around Dubai but a
well-equipped four-wheel
drive is required for more
remote surf spots

Other local breaks
Head south-west, deeper
into Oman and Yemen,
and who knows what you
may find on the shores of
the Arabian Sea

While you're there
No surf? Try sand surfing,
or a four-wheel safari
into the desert

OMAN AND DUBAI

Man oh man, surf in Oman...?

Even today, the Middle East is pretty much terra incognita as far as most
surfers are concerned, for various reasons including a harsh climate and forbidding
topography that makes travel difficult outside of major cities. There is also the
possibility of cultural clashes.

But if you can get around these little difficulties, surf may be found along the shores of
the Gulf of Oman and the Arabian Sea, and even in Dubai in the United Arab Emirates.
Should you find yourself in this part of the world with your board it's well worth searching
out a wave or two since the chances are you'll have them almost to yourself and the
water will be warm and welcoming.

Dubai is the focal point of the Middle Eastern surf scene, and is where various expats
have come together to form the kind of keen and enthusiastic surf club that only seems
to develop where the surf requires you to be keen and enthusiastic even to get into the
water in the first place.

Dubai, of course, has become synonymous with all that is excessive and bling about
twenty-first century lifestyles, so the fact that you can have the best fun on the beach for
free is a nice little anachronism that won't be lost on most surfers.

The waves around Dubai generally break over sand, as you might expect since they're
backed by a mighty desert, and they'll develop on the back of strong north-westerly
winds that blow virtually every day in winter and can produce waves of modest height but
no great shape or power – think onshore head high windswell on a reasonably good day.

You might thus conclude that this isn't anything to write home about, although at least
the water is warm. But a surf trip isn't always just about the waves, and surfing with the
somewhat bizarre backdrop of Dubai and the remarkable culture clashes that are part
and parcel of the city will undoubtedly make the experience memorable.

And if you want waves that might make you grin with pleasure as opposed to
amusement, you can take the 370-mile drive across to the Arabian Sea where the island
of Masirah off the Oman coast can on occasion show some very acceptable reef, point
and beach break set ups.

The waves here occur in the peninsula's sizzlingly hot summers and emanate from
southern hemisphere storms. They may have modest size and power, but they're often
messed up by the region's prevailing south-westerly winds so try and get them in the
early morning when conditions are more likely to be offshore.

One piece of gear you definitely won't need here is a wetsuit. Water temperatures can
get beyond 30°C (86°F) so you'll be doing well if you can keep the wax on your board.

Comoros
Islands

Malawi

Mozambique

Madagascar

Indian
Ocean

Difficulty
Intermediate – expert

Hazards
Sharks; shallow coral
reefs; remote;
political unrest;
poor communication
facilities; disease

Season
Year round, but May –
September best

Water temperature
25–29°C (77–84°F)

Wetsuit
Boardshorts and rash
vest; reef boots

Access
Very poor and very slow
to all coastlines; access to
outer reefs may only be
possible via boat

Other local breaks
Endless scope for
exploration locally or
try Madagascar to the
southeast

While you're there
On Grande Comoros
check out the colonial
architecture in the capital
Moroni, or hike to the
summit of the active
volcano Mt Karthala
(7,746 ft)

COMOROS ISLANDS

Tropical perfection – almost

It's possible that you may not have heard of the Comoros Islands, an archipelago
of four relatively small, angular volcanic land masses that sit in the Indian Ocean between
Madagascar and Mozambique.

That may be no bad thing. After all, it's rare to find there's a place with idyllic tropical
landscapes, glorious coastline and perfect azure blue waves that is so little known. But the
islands' remote location, difficulty of access, decades of political instability and extremely
hassly travel once there, along with the obvious poverty and disease suffered by many of
the inhabitants, have all conspired to ensure that the Comoros have never been top of
many people's holiday lists, with or without surfboards.

Of course all this means that, for those surfers who are adventurous enough to visit,
empty waves are virtually guaranteed. The main island of Grande Comoros (or Njazidja)
is the point of access and there are beach and reef breaks to be found here, but the best
documented spot is the vaguely triangular island of Anjouan, which has a long south-
westerly strip of reef fringed coastline that picks up solid south-westerly swells from the

high southern latitudes with remarkable consistency throughout the winter months.

Lefts and rights hurtle across shallow reefs, fanned by offshore trade winds that also push swell into the east coast, although this is clearly going to be onshore when the trade winds are blowing.

Cyclone swells also boom onto the north and east shores in summer, but these too are often accompanied by onshore or cross shore winds. Winter is the best time to visit anyway since it's far drier and noticeably cooler than summer.

Indeed, in many ways a winter visit to the Comoros Islands is just what the doctor ordered: a perfect tropical climate with the scent of native frangipani and ylang ylang hanging in the air; consistent, solid groundswell and powerful crystal clear waves; and each distant reef pass likely to have a left and right reeling off either side of it. Closer inshore, volcanic beaches fringed by palms offer turquoise barrels that perhaps no surfer has ever ridden.

You need a spirit of adventure to score this kind of surf perfection and it's unlikely a trip here will be without its hassles, whether they're to do with travel, health or communication. And there's also a healthy shark population living in the waters of the offshore Mozambique Channel to consider too.

So there's no real rush to get out here because it's not likely the Comoros Islands will be getting over surfed any time soon.

Tanzania

Indian
Ocean

Seychelles

Mozambique

Madagascar

Difficulty
Intermediate – expert

Hazards
Sharks; shallow coral
reefs; remote

Season
Year round, but May –
September best

Water temperature
20–26°C (68–78°F)

Wetsuit
Boardshorts and rash vest
in summer, shortie in
winter; reef boots

Access
Poor to most breaks
outside of main towns; a
boat or four-wheel drive
will often be needed

Other local breaks
The Comoros Islands
(see p50) to the north-
west offer more scope for
surf exploration

While you're there
Take a wildlife tour – this
is what the majority
of visitors come to
Madagascar for

MADAGASCAR

One of the world's biggest islands – and one of the least surfed

The world's fourth largest island, Madagascar is over two and a half times bigger than the UK. Yet only a handful of places here are surfed with any kind of regularity, with most being located in the south of the island.

One major reason Madagascar has stayed off the surfing map is its reputation for sharks, although the most sharky areas (for instance, the west coast and the north-east coast) can be avoided and you'll still score great waves. And the shark threat has probably been overemphasized in the past.

People are also put off by the difficulty of getting around. It's a hassle at times, with coastal roads often being rudimentary or non-existent, and accommodation options are extremely limited outside the main settlements.

So all in all there's still a bit of a frontier feel to surfing here, which means you can be pretty assured that you won't have to worry about sharing the waves with too many others. And waves there are aplenty, with the south of the island receiving consistent action year round from the surfer's friend, the Roaring Forties. This is particularly the case between May and September, when the winds are also predominantly offshore at the main spots, while December to March may see cyclone swells on the east coast.

There's also a good range of breaks. Around Fort Dauphin in the south-east, for instance, quality beach breaks such as those at Ambinamy Bay alternate with left and right hand reefs to the north, while on the south-west coast between Androka and Tulear there are some world class reef pass waves (for which you will need a boat; and surf yacht charters are available to the island).

The beautiful beach at Lavonono is the main draw for most surfers, however, with aquamarine beach and reef breaks peeling left and right onto smooth white sand beaches. There's also a surf camp here, where you may pick up some good local knowledge.

This part of Madagascar is perhaps not what you'd expect from a tropical island in terms of scenery, since the wet east coast and its lush rainforest vegetation is replaced by dusty, scrubby conditions on the drier west coast.

Perhaps the most exotic place of all to surf – if you can deal with the possibility of sharks – is at Sambava towards the northeast tip of Madagascar. Here you'll find a fine right hand rivermouth point, which gives long, fast rides amidst the evocative aroma of vanilla, thanks to Sambava place at the centre of the island's vanilla (and coconut) growing industry.

It is admittedly a long way to travel from the south coast to catch a wave, but unless you're on a surf boat charter it's well worth taking some time off to explore Madagascar. The people may be generally poor but they're a real delight to meet and inland the mountains rise to almost 10,000 feet, their slopes home to some of the world's rarest and most exotic creatures such as lemurs (this is the only place in the world that they exist in the wild), chameleons and the superbly monikored giant jumping rat!

Indian
Ocean

Madagascar

Mauritius

Réunion

Difficulty
Good intermediate –
expert

Hazards
Crowds and localism;
sharks; shallow breaks
over live coral; sea urchins

Season
Year round but May
– September most
consistent

Water temperature
24–28°C (75–82°F)

Wetsuit
Boardshorts and rash
vest; boots for protection
from reefs; a shortie
may be useful on
cooler days in winter

Access
Good to all of the
popular breaks

Other local breaks
None that aren't
shark infested

While you're there
Head inland to explore
the spectacular volcanic
peaks, some of which
are active

RÉUNION ISLAND

Perfect waves – apart from the sharks

In terms of drama, this place has it all: amazing aquamarine waves, spectacular
volcanic landscapes and consistent waves year round allowing wetsuit free surfing.

That's as long as you stay on the west side of Réunion. The east of the island is about
as uninviting as a tropical island could be for a surfer. Sharks galore and a wet and
unpleasantly humid climate are not likely to have anyone rushing there soon, even though
there are some decent point breaks to be surfed.

So, back to the west coast, where the sun is usually shining, the volcanic uplands
shrouded by clouds and a solid southwest groundswell hitting the reefs.

The quality peaks that race across the live coral below their glassy faces are actually
partly the result of those clouds swirling around the 10,000-feet peaks above, since the
rain that pours out of the clouds year round is channelled down to the coast. Over time
it has worn away gaps in the reef as the water flows out to sea and either side of these
'passes' you'll find waves peeling off left and right (but mainly left).

Indeed, Réunion's most famous wave is the picture perfect left of St Leu, which cracks
across the reef in front of the eponymous town with startling consistency and precision;

and, although it breaks some way out to sea (as do most of the island's waves), it's an easy, dry hair paddle out to the peak.

But that's where the easy bit ends. In common with virtually all of Réunion's waves, St Leu is fast and shallow, so you need to know what you're doing to surf it, and even more so because it's invariably busy and the locals are not known for suffering fools gladly.

Unfortunately for novice surfers, there are very few easy waves other than occasional, rare beach breaks such as those of the popular white sands of Roches Noire near the regional centre of St Gilles les Bains.

However, if you're an experienced surfer who likes a challenge and is looking to surf some truly classic tropical waves, you're sure to get a buzz out of Réunion. It's worth bearing in mind that, while the east coast of the island is particularly well known for its sharks, the west coast is not shark-free, and attacks on surfers have been recorded here. You can reduce the risk considerably by avoiding murky waters (particularly after a storm) and not surfing at dawn or dusk, as well as making sure you exit the surf if you get any cuts or nicks from the reef.

At the end of the day, somewhere in the local waters − and it may be some way off − there will be a shark or two. The chances that you'll get to meet one close up are very slim, but it's there nevertheless. And it will certainly add a frisson of additional excitement to all your wipeouts...

Botswana

Lesotho
South Africa
Durban

*Indian
Ocean*

Difficulty
Beginner – expert

Hazards
Crowds; sharks at beaches without nets; occasional street violence/hassles

Season
April – July

Water temperature
21–25°C (69–77°F)

Wetsuit
Shortie or 3/2 steamer in winter; boardshorts and rash vest in summer

Access
Good to all of the popular breaks

Other local breaks
Drive south and you'll eventually come to South Africa's surfing gem, Jeffrey's Bay; to the north are the relatively unexplored shores of Mozambique

While you're there
If you visit during peak winter surf season, consider heading to the Drakensburg Mountains to ski/board if you get a flat spell

DURBAN, NATAL, SOUTH AFRICA

South Africa's 'Surf City' has waves for everyone

Durban is one of the planet's few large cities that can justly claim to have world class surf of every shape and form. Whether you want fun beach breaks, hollow reefs, reeling points or booming big wave spots, you'll find them in or close to the city's shores.

In addition, Durban has all the attractions of one of the most vibrant and colourful cities in South Africa. It's a major tourist hub for both South Africans and overseas visitors, with a welcoming climate year round and warm waters in which to play, whether you're cruising on a longboard or scuttling around on a lid.

All this has made the city a focal point of South African surfing and results in a buzzing surf scene, plenty of competition for waves and a very high standard of wave riding, but if you can be bothered to drive a few miles north or south of Durban you'll find quieter waves for sure.

There is, of course, one more thing that Durban is known for: sharks. There's no getting away from the fact that you are not at the top of the food chain when you enter the

Indian Ocean off Durban, but you can take solace from the fact that all the city's beaches have shark nets so the chances of actually becoming part of the food chain are minimal. Outside the city, well, few beaches have nets so you have to take your chances.

There are a score or more eminently surfable breaks within the city limits, with standouts including the excellent and consistent beach breaks of North Beach and its neighbour Dairy Beach (note that there are daytime restrictions on surfing at North Beach in the summer tourist season but Dairy Beach has unlimited access); the renowned, expert-only thundering barrels of Cave Rock; and Snake Park Beach, which the locals have totally wired – you may struggle to score a good wave here but it's worth a visit to view the high standard of surfing on display.

If you decide to venture further afield, car hire is generally pretty cheap and will open up masses of waves to both the north and south. Standouts within 60 miles or so to the south include the quality right hand point breaks (Natal has relatively few lefts) of Green Point and The Spot; within 60 miles of the north of the city are a wide array of low tide breaks that pitch out fast and hollow over a mixed sand and reef bottom.

The best period for surf is April to July, when reassuringly consistent south-west swells pound the coastline, morning offshores are virtually guaranteed and the weather is like a (good) English summer. About the only downside is that you may need a summer steamer if you feel the cold.

Which is a pretty easy 'downside' to live with, really.

Mauritania

Dakar

Senegal

Mali

Atlantic Ocean

Difficulty
Beginner – expert

Hazards
Crowds; shallow reefs with urchins; sharks

Season
Year round, but autumn/ winter most consistent

Water temperature
18–27°C (64–80°F)

Wetsuit
2mm full suit in winter; boardshorts and rash vest in summer; boots useful for reefs

Access
Good

Other local breaks
Head north of Yoff for tens of miles of quiet beach breaks

While you're there
Dakar is a vibrant city day and night, with good nightlife; a visit to the former slave island and UNESCO World Heritage Site of Île de Gorée can be a sobering experience

DAKAR, SENEGAL

A great introduction to exotic African surfing

If you've never surfed warm water reefs in a tropical third world country before, Senegal is a good place to start. Good value package deals, surf camps catering for the less intrepid and waves to suit all levels of ability make this an attractive option and it's a wonder that the country hasn't featured more highly on the list of most surfers' 'must ride' locations. After all, the quality right hand reef break that reels across from the western tip of N'gor Island was featured in the classic surf movie 'Endless Summer' almost 50 years ago.

This break is one of the major attractions of the coastline around the capital city of Dakar, which sits on the Almadies Peninsula, Africa's westernmost point and, as such, is a location that is exposed to swells from almost every point of the compass.

N'gor Right is just one of a number of quality reef breaks, the primo spot being Ouakam on the peninsula's west coast, which, when it's on, produces top notch lefts and rights where getting barrelled is the order of the day.

All of these spots are within a cheap and easy taxi ride of the buzzing city centre, and all of them can pack a fair old punch as well as breaking over shallow, urchin festooned rocks, so they're best left to experienced surfers.

For newbies looking for a less daunting introduction the place to head for is Yoff Beach, a long strand that, even in these surfed out times, can turn up quiet peaks if you don't mind a bit of a tramp down the beach.

The best time to visit is in autumn/winter, when swells pour onto the coast from the north and north-west and, in the early part of the season, the south and south-west too, which means that there's always a good chance of getting offshore conditions. The slight downside to this is that you don't get to experience the boardshorts conditions of summer when the water can reach 27°C (80°F), but even the relatively cool 18°C (64°F) winter waves are considerably warmer than what most visitors are used to at home at this time of year — and those palm fringed beaches and the fascinating Franco-African culture are still there to add that touch of the exotic.

The French influence will be apparent out in the water, since many of the expat surfers in Dakar are from France and the burgeoning number of surf related businesses are often French owned.

Add to this a healthy population of local surfers and a smattering of travellers from other parts of the world and you have a pretty cosmopolitan surf culture. All a far cry from the 'Endless Summer' days when N'gor Right was surfed for the first time ever, but still enough to make Senegal a very tempting destination, especially in winter.

59

Difficulty
Beginner – expert

Hazards
Malaria; some pollution in
urban areas

Season
Year round, but May –
October most consistent

Water temperature
23–26°C (73–78°F)

Wetsuit
Boardshorts and rash vest;
shortie may be useful on
cooler/breezier days

Access
Good to most of the
popular breaks

Other local breaks
Togo and Ivory Coast
to either side of Ghana
remain relatively
unexplored but there's
plenty of scope for scoring
quality waves

While you're there
Take a guided tour of the
various slave forts along
the coast

GHANA

User friendly waves and exotic
West African shorelines

Long, sandy beaches interspersed by rocky headlands, palm trees waving in the
offshore breeze and consistent swells rolling ashore from storms way off in the southern
hemisphere mean there's a pretty good chance you'll score some quality surf time on a
visit to Ghana.

And if you're looking for a more relaxed kind of surf trip with easy beach breaks, no
crowd hassles and no shallow reefs to tear the arse out of your boardshorts, this is the
place to be.

The majority of the breaks in Ghana are user friendly beachies – the gently shelving
shoreline means that a lot of the oomph has been taken out of Ghana's swells by
the time they spend themselves on their final lurch to the shore, and although bigger
overhead waves are not uncommon, you're more likely to get fun surf that encourages
you to go for it and work on your technique without any real consequences when you
wipe out.

A classic example of this is Busua Beach towards the western end of the country's
short, south-facing coastline. Here you'll find one of the loveliest beaches in Ghana, all

white sand and shady palms, while enticing peaks break in the blue waters lapping against those sandy shores.

In fact, this is the epicentre of Ghana's slowly developing surf scene, with the only surf shop in the country and a handful of local and expat surfers enjoying the waves and the friendly vibe of one of Africa's most chilled out nations.

Either side of Busua are two more great breaks, Dixcove to the east, a consistent, slow breaking right hand point break located below an old slave fort, and Three Points to the west, another right point set beneath a lighthouse on the headland above. (Left hand points are in somewhat short supply in Ghana so goofies may find fault.)

You'll invariably arrive in the country through the capital of Accra, which also has waves on Labadi Beach. This is popular with both visitors and locals and is worth checking out, as is the city, but it won't give you the more relaxed experience you'll enjoy if you take the short journey west towards Busua Beach.

For northern hemisphere surfers, there are very obvious attractions to hitting Ghana in the winter, when wetsuit-free surfing is the order of the day and the only downside is that the surf tends to be less consistent, although on the plus side you do get the cool, dry Harmattan wind blowing at this time of year. As well as making life more comfortable, this also provides offshore conditions. (If you choose to visit between May and October, when the surf is more consistent, take an umbrella since this is the rainy season.)

Add to this a friendly local population, almost all of whom speak English, and it's hard to find a reason not to visit Ghana if you're an average surfer looking for some exotic warm waves in a fascinating country.

Sierra
Leone

Côte
d'Ivoire

Liberia

*Atlantic
Ocean*

Difficulty
Beginner – expert

Hazards
Some shallow breaks;
remote; part of the
developing world; dirty
water; malaria; disease

Season
May – October bigger
swells but worse weather;
November – April smaller
swells, better weather

Water temperature
26–28°C (78–82°F)

Wetsuit
Boardshorts and rash vest

Access
Decent access to breaks
in Robertsport and
Monrovia; other spots can
be a real mission to reach
and many, many breaks
remain undiscovered

Other local breaks
There is no end of surf
awaiting discovery in
Sierra Leone to the north
and along Liberia's
southern shores

While you're there
If you get the chance
to visit the bush there's
an amazing array of
wildlife to be discovered,
including elephants,
leopards and gorillas

LIBERIA

Hardcore travellers will find much to relish in this battered nation

It's probably a bit much to suggest that surfing may help to cure the ills of a nation like Liberia, which was torn apart by civil war for more than a decade up to the early years of the twenty-first century. Nevertheless, the small trickle of overseas cash that surfers bring with them, along with the camaraderie and cross-cultural understanding that the sport invariably engenders, can certainly do no harm.

That said, Liberia doesn't give up its surf riches readily – and riches there undoubtedly are. Top notch lefts and super fun beach breaks barrel ashore with satisfying consistency throughout the summer, but the rain also buckets down so intensely at times that you may wonder whether you're as dry in the surf as on the beach.

And when the rain eases off in winter and the winds go more offshore, the swell becomes smaller and less consistent, although not so much as to make a surf trip unviable.

So, the time you visit will depend on just how much damp and humidity you can handle. This, together with the strife of previous years, the West's image of the country as being part of the developing world, and the difficulty of travel, are all reasons for Liberia only latterly starting to register on the surfing map.

If you're adventurous enough to take the flight into the capital, Monrovia, and explore the country's 360-mile coastline, the pay off can be huge. You needn't be a total charger to enjoy the surf here, either.

The majority of known breaks to be found between Monrovia and the town of Robertsport in the north-west of the country are fun, warm beachies, which, unless breaking at some size, even novice wave riders can enjoy. These are interspersed with more challenging and often very long left point breaks that will flatter intermediates and be ripped apart by more advanced surfers.

Monrovia has a selection of readily accessible beach breaks, and similar conditions are to be found along the vast stretch of white sand between the capital and Robertsport, but it's the latter spot that is becoming the focal point for surfing in Liberia.

A handful of friendly locals, a selection of equally friendly breaks that only become intimidating on larger swells, and year round swells marching up from the South Atlantic mean that, if you can deal with the climate and the deprivation, you're almost certain to score a few good sessions on a visit here.

You'll also discover at least some sense of what it must have been like for pioneering surf travellers of the '60s and '70s when they stumbled across coastlines that had never before been surfed, particularly if you make the difficult journey away from the 'centres' of Liberian surfing.

Equatorial
Guinea

**São Tomé
and Príncipe** Gabon

*Atlantic
Ocean*

Difficulty
Intermediate – expert

Hazards
Shallow reefs; remote;
malaria; intense
equatorial sun

Season
May – October

Water temperature
26–28°C (78–82°F)

Wetsuit
Boardshorts and rash
vest; boots useful on
some reefs

Access
Decent road access to
most breaks on the south-
west and south coasts

Other local breaks
None

While you're there
Try whale watching;
summer coincides with
humpback whales passing
the island as they migrate
from lower latitudes
to tropical mating and
calving grounds

SÃO TOMÉ

Surf two hemispheres on the same day

Now, here's a unique surfing opportunity – the chance to take off on a wave in the
southern hemisphere and kick out in the northern hemisphere.

The left at Point Zero on the beautiful little tropical islet of Illhue das Rolas off the
southern tip of São Tomé may be the only break on Earth with this distinction, straddling,
as it does, the Equator.

There's no real need to make the short boat journey here from the main island since
there are plenty of quality waves on São Tomé too, but it does make for a good story to
tell when you get back home.

There again, just surfing on the former Portuguese colony of São Tomé is a good story
to tell, since to date not that many outsiders have ridden the waves here. But local kids
have been paddling out into the surf on makeshift wooden planks for who knows how
long; US surf traveller Sam George described meeting smiling, enthusiastic youngsters
doing their own thing in the waves on São Tomé when he visited in 2000, so it's a safe
bet that rudimentary 'surfing' has been taking place here for some time.

And a generous few of the trickle of modern surfers passing through the lush volcanic island in the first decade of the twenty-first century left their boards behind, so there are now a score or so local surfers who don't rely on the sides of old canoes or lengths of wooden door to catch the waves.

You'll find the local crew hanging out at Porto Alegre (Portuguese for 'Port Joy', and perhaps with good reason) at the southern tip of the island, where they probably don't know how lucky they are. A long, long right hand point break rolls ashore over a boulder and rock bottom, jade green wave faces glittering in the sunlight and offshore breezes rustling the palms above the point. With conditions like this it's no wonder the locals were happy to surf on lengths of waterlogged timber in the past.

Elsewhere on the island's south-west facing coast, there are several breaks accessed by the only decent stretch of coastal road. These vary from more challenging points breaks to easy beach breaks at Baia Coqueiro, all of which fire into action on summer's south-westerly swells. The waves don't tend to be excessively big but they are consistent.

São Tomé's drier west coast would also offer waves to the intrepid traveller, but access is slow and difficult so little is known about the surf hereabouts. But with the island's east coast offering a combination of consistent summer surf, a great summer climate and virtually guaranteed empty waves, is there any real need to explore further just yet?

Atlantic
Ocean

**Cape Verde
Islands** Senegal

Difficulty
Intermediate – expert

Hazards
Shallow reefs; sharp
volcanic rocks; urchins;
sharks; sunburn/
dehydration; airborne
windsurfers and
kitesurfers

Season
September – April

Water temperature
20–27°C (68–80°F)

Wetsuit
Shortie in winter;
boardshorts and rash vest
in summer; boots useful
for reefs

Access
Varies; some breaks
require a long walk or
four-wheel drive to access

Other local breaks
The nearest breaks to
Sal are a series of beach
breaks on the island of
Boa Vista

While you're there
Learn to kitesurf; or read
all those books you know
you ought to

CAPE VERDE ISLANDS
A blast from the past

Surfers of a certain age may remember what it was like to surf in the Canary
Islands before crowds and localism spoilt most of the fun. The Cape Verde islands provide
something of a taste of those Canarian early days, with similar waves, a similar climate
and similar desert landscapes but, as yet, without similar crowd issues.

The focal point of surfing in this archipelago of 15 islands some 300 miles off the coast
of Senegal is the island of Sal, although the neighbouring island of Boa Vista has waves,
as do São Tiago and Fogo to the south-west, São Nicolau to the west, and São Vicente
and São Antão at the north-west reaches of the archipelago. There are ferry services
between the islands if you feel the urge to explore any of them.

Sal isn't the prettiest of islands, being flat, dry, sun baked and frequently windy, but
when you see the turquoise barrels grinding ashore at Ponta Preta on its south-west
corner it will appear attractive enough. And hey, add warm water and hot sun and you
have a pretty winning combination.

This is generally regarded as the best wave on Sal, offering 200-yard rights that break
best in winter and may also be populated by windsurfers and kitesurfers – yes, also like
the Canaries, the wind chasers are a major feature of the scene here.

They're drawn by the trade winds that come dominantly from the north-east and
north, often bringing with them red dust from the Sahara Desert. While they can hold up
the waves nicely, there are times when they're strong enough to make paddling into the
wave difficult.

The best and most consistent waves are to be found on the west coast, thanks to the
combination of north-westerly swells and the offshore/crosshore trades, but that's not to
say a little exploration of the island's other shores won't turn up the goods. Be warned,
sharks are frequently seen on the east side of Sal, although there are no records of
surfers having been attacked.

'Exploration' is easy on Sal, especially if you have access to a four-wheel drive, and it
will almost certainly turn up quiet peaks, since most people stick to the main west coast
breaks like the aforementioned Ponta Preta, the lefts of Santa Maria or the long rights of
Monte Leão.

For those who like to either surf or do nothing, Sal is a fine option because if there are
no waves there really isn't that much else to do. Bring a good book or two and plenty of
sun cream, and chill out between swells. It's a perfectly acceptable way to spend a day –
check out the locals, they're well versed in the art of taking it easy and, as they say, 'When
in Rome...'

Florida, USA   **Great Abaco**

The Bahamas   **Eleuthera Island**

Atlantic Ocean

Difficulty
Intermediate – expert

Hazards
Shallow coral reefs;
urchins; sunburn

Season
November – April

Water temperature
22–27°C (71–80°F)

Wetsuit
Boardshorts and rash
vest; reef boots; shortie
may be useful on windy
days in winter

Access
Reasonable road access
to most breaks, although
more remote spots may
require four-wheel drive
or boat

Other local breaks
Cat Island and San
Salvador to the south of
Eleuthera also have waves

While you're there
There's some of the
best snorkelling in the
Bahamas here, especially
on Eleuthera

GREAT ABACO AND ELEUTHERA, BAHAMAS
The 'freedom' of the seas

The Bahamas have plenty of surf potential, sitting as they do in the south-west corner of the North Atlantic. Most of the outer chain of the 700 islands, islets and cays that make up the archipelago will pick up swell (although this is not the case for the main island, Andros, which is generally too sheltered).

We've focused here on just two of the bigger isles, Great Abaco and Eleuthera, towards the northern end of the archipelago. These are some of the easiest to access, they're large enough to have a decent range of breaks and there's enough to occupy you if it's flat (only around five per cent of the islands are inhabited and many are little more than rocky outcrops).

Each island shares warm, turquoise waters, which see very acceptable and quite consistent waves roll onto their eastern shores from North Atlantic storms, hence winter is the most consistent period. Hurricanes can also provide classic swells as long as they don't come too close to the islands, which can be a serious concern at times.

Great Abaco's breaks are generally a fun selection of left and right hand reefs, which can be shallow in places and may be a bit tricky to get in and out of but are certainly worth the hopping about over rock and coral. There's only one real beach break at Four Rocks, near the island's main settlement, Hope Town, which means that Great Abaco isn't ideal for novice wave riders despite the temptations of its gentle climate and chilled environment.

More adventurous surfers with access to a boat will also discover plenty of waves on the more exposed offshore cays, and this also applies to Eleuthera. This was the first island in the Bahamas to be colonized, by adventurers from England seeking religious freedom who settled here in 1647, and the island's name comes from the Greek word for freedom.

There's consequently a very tolerant and relaxed vibe on Eleuthera, where locals and visitors generally rub along together pretty well, even in the ever more crowded waves. (At holiday periods and when good swells are predicted, you should expect an influx of surfers from nearby Florida.) This is one of the biggest and most attractive islands in the Bahamas archipelago. ('Bahamas' is an anglicized form of the Spanish baja mer, or 'shallow sea', but this isn't strictly accurate since there's a 3,000-foot trench a mile or so offshore, which acts as a good magnet for east and north-easterly swells.)

Indeed, winter can see some fast and heavy swells booming onto Eleuthera's reef and beach breaks (the latter are very much in the minority) and since the island arcs around from north facing to south facing, it's well open to variations in swell direction.

And the best tip you'll get for surfing here? Before you paddle out for your first waves of the morning, breakfast on the local fruit – the pineapples are absolutely sensational and will keep you going all day!

Barbados

Grenada

Atlantic Ocean

Venezuela

Difficulty
Beginner – expert

Hazards
Shallow reefs; urchins and stonefish; intense sun

Season
January – May or September – November

Water temperature
26–28°C (78–82°F)

Wetsuit
Boardshorts and rash vest; boots useful for reef protection

Access
Decent road access to most breaks

Other local breaks
None

While you're there
Try the local rum, it's among the best in the world (Old Brigand's Ten Year Old is recommended by locals); but you may have to forget surfing the following day

BARBADOS

The best soup in the world

When nine-times world surfing champion Kelly Slater describes a place as having "one of the top three waves in the world" then you'd expect people to sit up and take notice.

Yet despite him bestowing this shining accolade on the aquamarine wall of water with the unlikely monikor of Soup Bowls that barrels across one of eastern Barbados' urchin infested reefs, this teardrop shaped outlier of the Windward Islands has yet to endure the heavy crowds and general brouhaha that so often go hand in hand with 21st century surfing.

Quite why this is so, who knows? And who cares? Certainly not the fortunate residents who live and surf there and epitomize the languid, laconic and laid back lifestyle of the West Indies.

These are dudes who have mastered the art of appearing chilled and approachable on land, while retaining a different kind of chill when in the water – no one really minds you surfing 'their' waves, but surf them with respect.

Barbados, of course, has a bit of a reputation for providing a glitzy, James Bond type of Caribbean experience, but that's the west coast where the silver sands and powder blue seas match the hair colour of many of the visitors.

Head across to the east coast and the tourist numbers rapidly fall away as you discover the 'real' Barbados, a land of sugar canes swaying in the sea breezes, monkeys screeching in the high palms and muscled Atlantic swells booming ashore to provide some of the best waves in the West Indies (or the world, if we're to believe Mr Slater).

One glance at a map and it's pretty obvious why Barbados is on the receiving end of such fine surf. As the most easterly and thus most exposed of the Windward Islands, it has an impressively wide swell window and is open to swells from north through to south-west, not to mention anything that is produced by the hurricanes that frequently thrash their way across the region.

There are more than 30 named breaks on the island as well as plenty of additional options for those prepared to explore, but you really don't need to make that effort, for, despite Barbados' accomplished local surf population, a steady trickle of visiting surfers, various surf schools and the surf holidays and surf tours offered on the island, there still seem to be enough waves to go around.

Even better, there are waves for all abilities, from the heavy barrels of Soup Bowls and Cattlewash on the east coast to a series of far mellower left hand points on the west coast and good beginner/intermediate breaks like Surfer's Point and Brandons on the south coast.

Nicaragua
Caribbean Sea
Costa Rica
Panamá

Difficulty
Intermediate – expert

Hazards
Some crowded line ups; shallow reef breaks; heavy waves; sharks and sea crocodiles; some theft in urban locations

Season
Winter usually has the best combination of swell and weather

Water temperature
24–28°C (75–82°F)

Wetsuit
Boardshorts and rash vest; boots for reefs

Access
Easy access to main breaks; more remote spots can be difficult to access and may require boat or four-wheel drive

Other local breaks
Panama to the south has heaps of top quality lineups

While you're there
You have to visit one or more national parks – Costa Rica has some of the richest and most colourful ecosystems and wildlife on earth

COSTA RICA, CARIBBEAN COAST

The right hand coast of this surf rich nation holds plenty of surprises

Costa Rica's Caribbean coast is less visited by surfers than the country's more famous Pacific shores, partly because it's more hassle to get here (although the journey through the spectacular rainforests of Costa Rica's highland interior is one to be relished rather than reviled) and partly because the coastline is considerably shorter than that of the Pacific to the west, so surf options are more limited.

But the tropical storms and hurricanes that lash the more northerly latitudes around Mexico can produce surprisingly big, powerful winter waves along the Caribbean coast, and these are often more challenging than the waves of the country's Pacific coast.

Most surfers will be drawn to the fast, barrelling reef break of Salsa Brava, the most heavily surfed spot along the coast but not a place for the inexperienced. The English translation is apt: 'wild (or strong) sauce'. This can be one of the biggest and heaviest breaks in the country, and the competition for waves is invariably fierce. There's an

intriguing mix of Caribbean and Rasta cultures onshore in the somewhat hippyish town of Puerto Viejo, which fronts the break. If you want to hang out with the local and travelling surf crowd, this is the place to be as the rest of the coast is relatively quiet, other than at the regional capital of Puerto Limón.

Here you'll find more challenging breaks, including various fast, heavy and shallow reef breaks to the north of the town, which the locals have wired. Treat them and the break with respect and you could have fun here. As for the sharks that are seen in the area from time to time, well, how you treat them is up to you.

In between Puerto Limón and Puerto Viejo is a long stretch of grey sandy beach that has limited potential for surf since the waves don't tend to have great shape, the water is often cloudy due to runoff from several rivers and there are known to be sharks and possibly even crocodiles in the grey-brown waters.

If that doesn't sound too appealing, beach breaks such as those off Manzanillo to the south of Puerto Viejo can offer up an appealing variety of waves, although even these can be remarkably punchy. For the more adventurous, a trip towards the Panamanian border may well turn up a peak or two with no more than a handful of surfers out, if that.

You may need a boat to access some of the more remote breaks, or it may involve a short trek through jungle that comes right down to the coast. Look upon that as a positive; you might spot anything from tree frogs to howler monkeys as you hoik your board through the brush,.

And the sapphire blue waves that you'll encounter at the end of your trek will surely make it all worthwhile.

Nicaragua

● **Costa Rica**

Panamá

Pacific Ocean

Difficulty
Beginner – expert

Hazards
Some crowded lineups;
shallow reef breaks;
sharks and sea crocodiles
(no reported attacks);
insects and sea lice; some
theft in busier locations

Season
Year round, although
winter usually has best
combination of swell
and weather

Water temperature
26–28°C (78–82°F)

Wetsuit
Boardshorts and rash vest

Access
Easy access to main
breaks; more remote
spots can be difficult to
access and may need
four-wheel drive or boat

Other local breaks
Nicaragua to the north
and Panama to the
south have plenty of
top quality lineups

While you're there
Look out for sea turtles,
as many beaches are
nesting sites

COSTA RICA, PACIFIC COAST

A wealth of world class waves – but don't expect to get them to yourself

Costa Rica's popularity as a surf destination is more than amply deserved but it doesn't necessarily mean all the waves here are busy waves. The predictable year–round surf of the Pacific coast has been a magnet for decades for surfers drawn to the pura vida (literally 'pure life' or more commonly 'cool life') lifestyle of this stunningly lovely country.

More readily accessible than the Caribbean, there are enough quality beach, point and beach breaks along Costa Rica's Pacific coast to keep you happy for a lifetime.

Some of the finest waves are to be found in the Guanacaste region, which has amazingly consistent surf year round at spots such as the superb right hand point break of Ollie's and the equally good beach break of Playa Naranjo, while a little south of here is the popular Tamarindo area with a fine range of breaks to suit every level of surfer.

South again, you'll come to one of the focal points of Costa Rican surfing at Playa Hermosa. Easily reached from the capital of San José and close to the busy town of Jaco, there are some excellent and very consistent beach breaks along this long stretch of beach, which help to spread out the region's inevitably busy surf crew.

This area won't be to everyone's taste with its surf camps, surf bars and surf hostels, but you can easily escape all that by continuing south to Golfo Dulce at the southern tip of the country, where standout spots include the long, long left hand point break of Pavones and its mirror image right of Pan Dulce in the far south.

In between and even around the above mentioned breaks are a host of lesser known spots. These are likely to be less populated and will turn up waves to appeal to everyone, from double or triple overhead boomers to mellow little beach breaks, and a number of surf camps have been set up along the coast here to introduce beginners to the sport.

This means you'll find a fair old league of nations out in the water, on the beaches and in the bars, which, along with the laid back and friendly approach of most locals, results in the easy going vibe for which Costa Rica is known. This makes for a great introduction to Central American surfing, whether you're planning a couple of weeks' escape from the northern hemisphere winter or a longer surfari taking in the equally surf rich nations to either side.

Caribbean Sea

Costa Rica

Panamá

Columbia

Pacific Ocean

Difficulty
Intermediate – expert

Hazards
Some crowded breaks;
urchins and shallow reefs;
large tidal range; theft
in urban areas; malaria;
disease; intense heat
and humidity

Season
Pacific:
March – June
Caribbean:
December – April

Water temperature
26–28°C (78–82°F)

Wetsuit
Boardshorts and rash
vest; boots for reefs

Access
Good road access to the
most popular breaks;
others may require four-
wheel drive or boat

Other local breaks
Offshore islands on
both coasts offer good
waves if you can arrange
boat access

While you're there
Check out the amazing
highlands of the Parque
Nacional Volcán Barú,
home to Panama's
highest peak (11,400 ft)
and its most famous
mountain trail

PANAMA

The best of both worlds on Panama's Pacific and Caribbean coasts

One of the banks in Panama's Bocas del Toro region used to sport a sign on the door advising 'No Arms'. Whether this remains now that the area is being opened up to tourism is doubtful, but it gives a clichéd yet inaccurate reflection of how Panama is often perceived. In fact, the people are as warm and colourful as the waters you come here to surf.

Running like a long curved spine between the Pacific and Caribbean Ocean, Panama offers waves on two totally different shorelines and, unlike neighbouring Costa Rica, it's not such a mission to get from one to the other. You can travel from the Pacific to the Caribbean (and vice versa) in a couple of hours. That said, general travel here is not so straightforward as it is in Costa Rica due to poor roads.

The country's surf spots are varied and numerous enough to provide something for everyone, with one of the main attractions being the flawless point breaks of the Pacific coast. The focal point here is the Peninsula de Azureo, although this is by no means the only stretch of the Pacific coast where you'll find waves.

However, if you home in on this bulge of the country that thrusts out into the ocean to collect monotonously consistent south and south-west groundswells, the chances are you'll want to stick around thanks to the superb rights and left at spots such as Punta Brava and La Punta by the town of Santa Catalina at the peninsula's southern tip.

If these get too busy for you, try checking out the well mapped selection of points and reefs to the north-west around Remedios; alternatively, there are stacks of waves to be found towards hectic Panama City, although these will invariably be busy and may be polluted.

From Panama City, however, it's but a short leap across to the Caribbean coast via the main highway to Colón, where the adventurous can look at hiring a boat to access the fine reefs of Isla Grande to the east, for instance. Or you can hang a left and take the long, hot drive west to the spitting barrels of the spectacular and increasingly popular archipelago of Bocas del Toro. Here, ten beautiful tropical islands offer a range of magnificent breaks from beachies to reefs and points and, unlike on the Pacific coast, lefts predominate.

The prime surf season for each coastline varies, with the Pacific at its best in spring/ early summer and the Caribbean in winter/spring, while the short dry season, which is the best time to travel, is from December to April. So, time it right and you can get the best of all worlds by hitting Panama in early spring as the two peak surf seasons coincide and the weather is at its best – perfect!

Gulf of
Mexico

Guatemala

Honduras

El Salvador

Pacific Ocean

Difficulty
Beginner – expert

Hazards
Some crowded breaks;
urchins and shallow rocks;
sea lice at times;
theft; pollution,
malaria; disease

Season
Year round, but March –
October biggest and most
consistent

Water temperature
27–28°C (80–82°F)

Wetsuit
Boardshorts and rash
vest; boots for reefs

Access
Good road access to the
most popular breaks;
others may require four-
wheel drive or boat

Other local breaks
Head east to Nicaragua for
more of the same

While you're there
Discover the 22-mile
Ruta de las Flores
through the heart of
coffee country where the
wildflowers run amok
from October to February
and there's great hiking,
horseback riding and
mountain biking

EL SALVADOR

It's all right in regular foot surf paradise

Surf explorer Craig Peterson first recorded the classic point breaks of El Salvador
in Surfer magazine in the early '70s, describing how he would "idly watch a lip crystallize
and fall like a slow-motion film" as he paddled out at an unnamed spot, and how there
were probably several more such spots within 12 miles in either direction, but "we'll
never know".

Well, the whole world knows now that El Salvador, despite having the shortest coastline
in Central America, also has some of the finest right hand point breaks in the world, not to
mention a highly commendable smattering of beach and reef breaks too.

Along the country's 200-mile Pacific coast you'll find dozens of renowned breaks, from
the world famous right hand point of Punta Roca in La Libertad, with rides of 200 yards
or more over its rocky, urchin spiked sea floor, to miles of empty sandy beaches facing
directly into the firing line of phenomenally consistent south and south-west swells.

In fact it's rare to get a totally flat day in El Salvador and, although summer is the

main season, with waves regularly head high and often considerably bigger, even the less consistent winter dry season will provide you with more good waves in a month than many other so called surf spots get in a year, along with easier travelling conditions.

Should the unusual happen and your break of choice fail to show, head to Zunzal, a right hand point break a few miles west of La Libertad, which seems to have surf when everywhere else is flat.

Getting around by road isn't that easy, especially in the east of El Salvador and, in fact, access to a boat will pay huge dividends if you want to discover your own breaks. But there are surf camps and surf tours that will guide you to the best breaks on any given swell if you haven't got the time or patience to do it yourself.

If you do choose to go it alone, now that word of El Salvador's marvellous surf is well and truly out you can no longer expect to surf in glorious solitude as did Peterson four decades ago.

If you stick to the better known and more popular spots, such as the easy La Paz in La Libertad or the beach breaks at Los Cabanos beside the country's main port of Acajutla, the locals will be all over it, especially at weekends and holidays. However, there are long stretches of beautiful tropical coastline in between the main breaks and especially east towards Nicaragua, where you'll find empty peaks rolling ashore as they have been since long before Craig Peterson discovered this surf paradise.

México

México City

Puerto Escondido

Pacific Ocean

Difficulty
Beginner – expert

Hazards
Crowds; insects; some thefts and muggings reported; dodgy police

Season
Year round, but summer most consistent

Water temperature
26–28°C (78–82°F)

Wetsuit
Boardshorts and rash vest

Access
Good

Other local breaks
Other breaks in the area include the point breaks at La Punta and the beach breaks of Colotepec, both a few miles east

While you're there
You'll probably want to party, as Puerto Escondido is a major holiday resort, but maybe check the surf forecast first so you don't wake up to perfect waves when you have a hideous hangover

PUERTO ESCONDIDO, MEXICO

Fast, heavy, big and hollow – no wonder it's called 'Mexico's Pipeline'

The comparisons to Pipeline are now a pretty hackneyed part of the Puerto Escondido scene, but they are nevertheless justified and all the more remarkable when you consider that this is a beach break rather than a reef break.

That has both good and bad points. What is good is that, on smaller swells, it gives less experienced surfers the chance to experience the kind of raw ocean power that is normally reserved for shallow reef breaks. But bear in mind that the wipe outs will be just as heavy as a reef break, and even sand can give you a good pummelling if you're smashed onto it by a wave as powerful as Puerto Escondido.

What is not so good is that paddle outs can be a nightmare on bigger swells, and there's no guarantee that the banks will be working at their optimum at any given time. Close outs are common as swells get larger and this can lead to awfully frustrating sessions when you just can't get a good ride of any length.

But when it all comes together, this famous Mexican wave will have you whooping for joy as you drop smoothly in, crank a hard right turn (the best waves tend to be rights) and race along a jade green face that's doing its best to catch up with you and throw an arc of Pacific Ocean over your head. Yes, barrels are the order of the day at Puerto Escondido, as anyone who has ever seen a surf mag feature on the place will know.

Indeed, you'd be forgiven for thinking that every wave that ever breaks here is a classic keg. Much of the time this is indeed the case, but bear in mind that the wave can often be blown out in summer and from late morning onshore winds will invariably mess things up whatever the time of year.

But just what is it that allows Puerto Escondido to bear comparison with Hawai'i's finest? Well, a deep water trench off the shores of Zicatela Beach on which the wave breaks funnels powerful swells straight out of the Pacific, where they lurch onto the shallow sand bars to rise up into mighty walls of water that have little choice but to transmute into deep, hollow pits.

Waves of this quality are always going to be quite busy if not downright crowded, but paddle out and you'll almost certainly catch one of the more memorable rides. And the popularity of Puerto Escondido and the relative ease of access make it a good introduction to surfing in Mexico, especially if you're on surfari. Hit the booming barrels at Zicatela Beach first, then head off to the country's more remote breaks – it must be the right thing to do, thousands of others have followed this route over the years.

México

Guadalajara

Colima

Acapulco

Pacific Ocean

Difficulty
Beginner – expert

Hazards
Some crowded lineups; sharks; insects; tough climate; some thefts and muggings reported; dodgy police; stomach bugs

Season
Year round, but summer most consistent

Water temperature
26–28°C (78–82°F)

Wetsuit
Boardshorts and rash vest

Access
Easy access to most main breaks; more remote spots can be difficult to access

Other local breaks
Head south to Oaxaca (p80) for more world class surf

While you're there
Take a trip inland to the Nevado de Colima National Park with its two volcanoes: the extinct Nevado de Colima (13,780 ft); and the active Volcan de Fuego de Colima (12,530 ft), which can be climbed as long as it's showing no signs of activity

COLIMA AND NORTH-WEST MICHOACAN, MEXICO

Big, consistent swells year round for the adventurous traveller

In many ways this part of Mexico has the perfect surf set up, with a combination of phenomenally consistent swells, relatively uncrowded waves and low cost living making it a particularly good option for surfers looking for a touch of exotic warm water surfing on the cheap.

In fact, there's something of an embarrassment of riches here. Summer and autumn in particular can have so much big, powerful surf that less experienced surfers could find themselves trying to find somewhere small enough to surf. (That said, this is the wettest period and not ideal for travelling.)

As with so much of Mexico's 2,500 miles of swell pounded Pacific coastline, the Colima and Michoacan region receives waves from a combination of perfectly lined up southern hemisphere summer ground swells, late summer/autumn hurricanes and northern hemisphere winter storms, and with winds that are either non-existent or dominantly offshore it could hardly be better.

You'll probably be arriving here via the airport at Manzanillo, from which you can access a range of quality waves such as the world class beach breaks of Pascuales and Boca de Apisa; or head across the border into Michoacan state for more of the same at San Juan de Alima, which also has a good right hand point break on bigger swells.

Travelling south and deeper into Michoacan becomes a little more of an adventure, as many of the breaks can only be accessed down dirt tracks for which a four-wheel drive vehicle is pretty essential, and there have in the past been incidents when tourists have stumbled across drug trafficking operations in the bush with far from pleasant outcomes. So it pays to use caution and maybe get some advice from local surfers about where you should and shouldn't visit.

One spot you should definitely hit – and where there are unlikely to be any bandito issues – is Guagua, with its inspiring set up of relatively empty left and right river mouth breaks. By now you'll be well south of Manzanillo and things will be increasingly hardcore. There will be fewer travelling surfers and locals, which is obviously a good thing, but there will also be more likelihood of hassles, which may be anything from floods and washed out roads in the rainy season to dodgy Federales or pesky mosquitos.

If you head onwards, however, the pay off can be worth it at spots such as Barra de Nexpa at Calla de Campas, where quality rights and lefts are to be found at the mouth of the Rio Nexpa.

At this point any surfer worth their salt will keep going, since Puerto Escondido (see p80) is starting to loom faintly on the horizon, but if the prospect of further slogging it along MEX200 doesn't appeal, that's no big deal – you'll already have scored some of Mexico's best waves and probably had an adventure or two en route.

San Diego
USA
Tijuana
México
Baja
Peninsula
Pacific Ocean

Difficulty
Beginner – expert

Hazards
Some crowded lineups;
jellyfish; poisonous
insects; some theft in
urban areas; sunburn
and dehydration; hordes
of partying tourists in
Los Cabos at holiday
weekends

Season
Year round

Water temperature
23–28°C (73–82°F)

Wetsuit
Shortie; boardshorts
and rash vest

Access
Easy access to all main
breaks; more remote
spots can be difficult
to access

Other local breaks
The Mexican mainland
(accessible by ferry from
La Paz) has no end of
world class surf

While you're there
It's worth heading north
to check out the inland
mountains of Sierra de
le Laguna, or try a sea
kayaking trip in the Sea of
Cortez from La Paz

BAJA PENINSULA, MEXICO

This dusty desert peninsula has a wealth of surf riches

The Baja Peninsula is the world's longest peninsula, and the entire 750 miles of its western side is washed by the Pacific Ocean so there's surf aplenty along its desert shores.

The northern section of this long finger of scrub and cactus (with the harsh climate and landscape that implies) is popular with Californian surfers attempting to escape the crowds of their homeland, although they tend to import that very problem of busy lineup to the more accessible spots, but numbers in the water will thin out as you continue south until you reach the southern tip of the peninsula.

Here the attractions of warmer water, hot sunshine, consistent swell and a good range of breaks to suit all abilities make this one of Mexico's most popular surf areas, with the focal point being around the towns of Cabo San Lucas and San José del Cabo, known collectively as Los Cabos. Even so, spots such as Costa Azul at San José have the kind of fast aquamarine walls that will tempt you in, however busy it is in the lineup.

If you want to escape the worst of the crowds you should drive north a little along the MEX1 highway and look out for dusty tracks and trails heading down to the Pacific. These will lead you to spots such as the laid back right at Cerritos, where campervans from all over North America are pulled up above the break, or nearby Pescadero and its quality reef breaks.

There's also the option of exploring. If you have a four-wheel drive vehicle you never know what you may find at the end of the more remote trails, although both you and your vehicle should be set up to deal with desert conditions.

Another option when really big swells roll ashore from regional tropical storms and cyclones is the beautiful coastline of the Sea of Cortez on the east side of the peninsula. Regarded more as a windsurfing and kiteboarding destination, this is the richest body of sea water on Earth; whales, manta rays, sea lions and no end of brightly coloured tropical fish are just a few of the underwater attractions. Amongst its rarer jewels are a variety of excellent right hand point breaks at spots such as Shipwrecks, Nine Palms and Los Frailes.

The waves tend to get smaller as you head north up the shores of the Sea of Cortez, however, and if it does go flat you can't drive immediately west to check out the Pacific coast, unfortunately, as road access across the desert is limited by the harsh and rugged landscape.

Oahu

Hawai'i

Pacific Ocean

Difficulty
Expert

Hazards
Fast and heavy waves;
swells can increase in
size very quickly; sharp
shallow reefs; intense
crowds and localism;
heavy rips on big swells;
occasional car theft

Season
October – March

Water temperature
24–27°C (75–80°F)

Wetsuit
Boardshorts and rash
vest; boots useful for reef
protection; shortie useful
for early mornings and
windy days

Access
Good road access to
most breaks

Other local breaks
South Shore, Oahu

While you're there
It will get so big, or you
will get so tired, that you
won't want to surf all the
time, so take a camera
and capture some of the
world class action on film

OAHU NORTH SHORE, HAWAI'I

Intense waves in every sense of the word

Oahu's North Shore has been the yardstick by which the world's surfers measure
their worth for five decades. Even the 21st century's new contenders for the crown of
World's Most Challenging Wave, such as Teahupoo (p30), Shipsterns Bluff (p194) or
Mullaghmore (p178) can't compete with this fabled stretch of coastline.

This isn't because these 'new' waves are lacking in size, power and ferocity. It's because,
in a strip of oceanfront real estate just over six miles long, the North Shore has everything
these other breaks offer, and has it to excess.

Waves like Pipeline, Sunset and Waimea are synonymous with surfing, even for non
surfers. Can there be an individual in the Western world who has not seen one or more
of these waves – whether in a movie or magazine, or advertising a credit card or a beer –
and not recognized in them the sheer raw power and beauty of nature?

For a surfer, it's not just about the challenge and thrill of taking on these and other
renowned breaks. There's also the history and culture of the sport that is integral to
this part of the world. Surfing today would not be what it is, had not the likes of Greg
'Da Bull' Noll had the sheer balls to paddle out and take on Pipeline in the early '60s
(having also pioneered 30-ft Waimea in 1957), and show that a wave that people once
thought impossible to ride could indeed be surfed. Fifty years on, the image of Noll in his
trademarked striped boardshorts, standing on the beach before a booming Pipeline swell,
is still one of surfing's most iconic.

Today, of course, the 18 or so named breaks that make up the North Shore are awash
with fibreglass every winter, as huge, long period North Pacific swells smash into the
shores of this volcanic island, which rears up out of thousands of feet of deep blue Pacific.
There's nothing to stop that power unwinding on the lava reefs that fringe the golden sand
shores, and there's nothing (other than the world's finest lifeguards) to stop anyone of any
ability paddling out into that surf.

You will find you're not just in competition with nature, however; you'll be in
competition with many of the world's best pro surfers, too, as well as a sizeable crew of
locals, a good number of who are just as good as the pros but choose not to be part of
the contest scene.

Then there is the fact that the locals don't suffer fools gladly – in fact, they don't suffer
them at all, and no one is going to hand you a wave if they can get it first. All of this
makes snagging a good ride on the North Shore in winter a pretty notable achievement
in itself.

If all this proves too much, there's Oahu's South Shore, which is easier to surf. Well – a
little bit easier.

Honolulu **Maui**

Hawai'i

Pacific Ocean

MAUI, HAWAI'I

Hawai'i's other North Shore

Difficulty
Novice – expert

Hazards
Fast and heavy waves; swells can increase in size very quickly; sharp shallow reefs; intense crowds and localism; heavy rips on big swells; occasional car theft

Season
November – February for north shore; May – August for south shore

Water temperature
24–27°C (75–80°F)

Wetsuit
Boardshorts and rash vest; boots useful for reef protection; shortie useful for early mornings and windy days

Access
Good road access to most popular breaks

Other local breaks
See Oahu (p86)

While you're there
On a massive winter swell, take a pair of binoculars and check out the action at Jaws from the cliffs above; or hire a mountain bike for some good off road action

To some extent, the Hawai'an chain's second largest island plays second fiddle to Oahu, but that can be to your advantage as it means it doesn't get quite as busy as its more famous neighbour.

That said, Maui doesn't have the consistency of surf that Oahu enjoys – but it does have equally heavy locals. Respect for the local huis is of the essence but, act graciously in the surf, and you'll get waves to remember.

In recent years, Maui has become famous for the tow-in spot Jaws, where a behemoth of a wave grinds across a distant reef to the north-east of Hookipa on monster swells, banging into the island's north shore to produce wave faces of 30–50 ft or more.

You need tow-in skills and all the associated equipment to surf here, and whilst it's become a bit of a zoo in recent years, Jaws should in no way be taken lightly. This is one wave that can easily kill or injure.

For most of us, there's more than enough challenge to be had in legendary breaks such as Honolua Bay on the island's north-west tip, which picks up winter's north and north-easterly swells and offers a very fast, very hollow and very crowded right hand point break of world class quality. You may struggle to catch a wave here since competition is heavy, but if you do it'll be worthwhile.

While the most powerful and most consistent surf tends to be found on the north-west shores of Maui, there are also some fine breaks to be had on the south facing coast, but these tend to be smaller and work in the summer when less common south-west swells hit the island. The good news is that these swells often come in conjunction with predominantly offshore winds.

Ma'alaea is the best known spot – hardly surprising, since it's one of the world's fastest rights, where it's as much a case of racing the lip to see how far down the line you can get as actually expecting to make it to the end. There's added excitement if and when you do wipe out, since the reef is shallow and sharp and may extract a price for your ride.

Less experienced surfers can also enjoy Maui as the island offers a number of less intimidating beach breaks, such as The Pali just west of Ma'alaea and S-Turns near Honokowai. Even so, as is always the case in the Hawai'ian islands, the power of the waves, even mellow beginner's waves, is not to be underestimated and will invariably be greater than what you're used to at home.

After all, the Hawai'ian chain is the most isolated and exposed archipelago in the world and open to every ripple that moves through the Pacific. Which is why it's the home of surfing, of course.

Paris

France

Bay of Biscay

Marseille

● Hossegor

Mediterranean Sea

Spain

Difficulty
Beginner – expert

Hazards
Crowds; currents and rips on bigger swells

Season
Year round

Water temperature
13–22°C (55–72°F)

Wetsuit
Steamer and boots in winter; shortie or boardshorts in summer

Access
Easy road access to all main breaks

Other local breaks
Head south to the world class left at Mundaka (p92) or north to the similar but slightly colder and less consistent beach breaks of La Côte Sauvage

While you're there
If the surf goes flat, head inland to the nearby Pyrenees for some great hiking, mountain biking and skiing

HOSSEGOR AND LES LANDES, FRANCE

One good session here and you'll understand why south-west France is the home of European surfing

Is there a surfer around who has visited France and not surfed Hossegor? The deep water channel just offshore of France's surf capital funnels in powerful swells from the Bay of Biscay. At their finest, these translate into gorgeous aquamarine barrels booming onto the sandy shores as a warm summer wind whisks their tops off. It's harder to imagine a better surf experience.

Add to that the great selection of bars and restaurants in the area, surf boutiques galore for those who want to splash their euros around and an eclectic mix of surf frenzied visitors from around the world, and few would argue that the Hossegor region is not the focal point of European as well as French surfing.

Indeed, at peak season in late August and September a whole rash of pro surf contests descend on the surrounding coast and if you're not a surfer you're very much out of place, whether on the beach or on the street.

Of course this won't appeal to everyone, but surf mania can be avoided easily enough with a short drive north. What is essentially one long golden beach extends for over 150 miles from Cap Breton in the south to the mouth of the River Gironde in the north, and all of it picks up pretty much the same swell as Hossegor – but without the crowds.

This general region, known as Les Landes, has been surfed since the '60s and many local families will have three generations riding the waves, while British surfers in particular have used the area's warm, clean waves for over four decades as a refuge from the cold, wet and onshore conditions that they're used to. So as a surfer, more than anywhere else in Europe, you really do feel at home here, even if you can't speak French. (English is the lingua franca amongst surfers here anyway.)

Despite all this, you can still explore the region and discover your own break. In between access points to the coast are long stretches of virtually empty shoreline, reached down sandy dirt roads and winding paths through cool green forests and over hot dusty dunes. If you're happy to take your chances and venture down one of these quiet trails, you may just find your own perfect beach break barrelling ashore in glorious solitude.

It can be difficult to find such breaks for a second time though – the dirt roads all look so similar and the sand banks can change their shape on bigger swells and storms, so the peak you surfed one day may no longer be there the next – but isn't it great to know that even in Europe's most popular surf zone there are still waves to be discovered?

Not to mention some very fine wine and food when the sun sinks beneath the horizon...

Difficulty
Expert

Hazards
Possible crowds; heavy wave with currents and rips on bigger swells

Season
Year round

Water temperature
12–20°C (53–68°F)

Wetsuit
Steamer and boots in winter; 3/2 steamer or shortie in summer

Access
Good road access

Other local breaks
There are beach breaks at Laga on the east side of the river mouth on smaller swells; to the west is the big wave spot of Menakoz

While you're there
Head into nearby Bilbao for a taste of Basque city life and a visit to the fascinating Guggenheim Museum; or San Sebastian to the east has some of the best tapas bars and clubs in northern Spain

MUNDAKA, NORTHERN SPAIN

A legendary wave in a legendary landscape

Ah, the legendary lefts of Mundaka. What a shame they only really break properly on a few days a year. But then, too much of a good thing would never do...

When Mundaka is at its finest it is arguably one of the world's greatest lefts; a fast, steep, barrelling wave that is a challenge even for the best. You need the right combination of swell, tide and wind, and ideally not too many people in the water, to catch this Basque beauty at its optimum.

That combination goes thus: a northwest swell over five feet in height; a southerly offshore wind; and the tide on low and rising. That's not to say you won't find a wave here with variations of these conditions, but if you get all three of these fundamentals in alignment then you're in business.

What makes Mundaka even more special is the quality and length of this classic wave at the mouth of the River Gernika. On a big swell, a 200-yard plus screamer of a ride is quite possible, starting with a vertiginous, angled take off, a tuck into the barrel and then foot to the floor and pump hard and high to race the lip and make at least two fast inside sections.

If you make it all the way down the line you're bound to want to paddle out for more, and even this is easy when Mundaka is on its best behaviour as there's a powerful rip current taking you back out to sea courtesy of the river. In fact, the best conditions often occur when the river is in full flow after the heavy rains that are frequent in the foothills of the Pyrenees, rising inland in folds of green.

In fact, Mundaka's location also contributes towards making it a special spot. The river mouth and estuary are lovely coastal features, while the hills and mountains inland are some of the least explored in Europe. The nearby village of Gernika is well known as the subject of Picasso's 1937 painting 'Guernica' that depicts the bombing of the town by German and Italian planes during the Spanish Civil War.

It would be nice to think that nowadays the nearest thing you'll get to bombs hereabouts are only the huge north-west swells, but this is the Basque heartland and very occasionally the Basque separatist movement ETA has let off explosive devices in the area. The chances of becoming involved in such incidents are miniscule though, and should in no way prevent you from checking out the wave at Mundaka and the fascinating Basque culture that it's a part of. That you'll be sharing the surf with a bevy of hot locals and travellers from around the world goes without saying, but Mundaka is a quintessential part of the European surf experience and one that you should certainly try and catch if you're in the area.

Bay
of
Biscay

Portugal

Ericeira   Spain

Lisbon

Difficulty
Intermediate – expert

Hazards
Possible crowds; heavy
waves; sharp shallow
reefs; sea urchins; strong
rips and currents on
bigger swells

Season
Year round

Water temperature
13–18°C (55–64°F)

Wetsuit
4/3 steamer and boots
in winter; 3/2 steamer
or shortie in summer

Access
Good road access to
some breaks; others
will require a hike

Other local breaks
Peniche to the north
has a selection of
world class breaks

While you're there
Head into nearby Lisbon
or take in the sites at the
historic city of Sintra

ERICEIRA, PORTUGAL

One of many gems along this thundering coastline that offers waves for all tastes

Portugal's Atlantic coast is bejewelled with an array of sapphire green peaks to suit everyone from beginner to big wave charger, and there is no better base for making the most of what the country has to offer than the coastal town of Ericeira, which has for over three decades been at the centre of the Portuguese surf scene.

Once an archetypal sleepy fishing village flanked by a deserted coastline of low cliffs and small bays, in recent years Ericeira has discovered the varied joys of tourism. What a handful of in-the-know surfers were aware of 30 years ago has now become common knowledge, partly due to the area being the venue of regular international contests in recent years.

Surprisingly, given this and the fact that the funky capital city of Lisbon is only 20 miles to the south, the selection of fast, tubing point and reef breaks and more mellow beach breaks to be found around Ericeira is big enough that crowds aren't always a problem, especially if you're happy to get off the beaten track a little.

That said, spots such as the easily accessible and regular contest site of Ribeira d'Ilhas are always popular but, with this coastline's consistent year round swell and regular offshore conditions, that's only to be expected.

When that swell gets big, the right-hand reef at Coxos is the place to head for – undeniably one of the Europe's finest waves. It's also a great place for viewing the action if you'd rather not take your chances with double or triple overhead waves.

The main concentration of breaks is to be found in a mere three-mile strip to the north of Ericeira. In addition to the above named spots, there's a fantastic selection of breaks varying from the Sunset-like behemoths of São Lourenço at the northern tip of the area to the dangerously shallow grinding reef break of the well named Reef just outside the town.

Most of the breaks are fast, shallow and heavy and are out of bounds to inexperienced surfers, who should head further south to the somewhat more forgiving breaks of Cascais and Estoril, but crowds are inevitable this close to Lisbon.

Many visiting surfers are surprised at the water temperature along this coast, given Portugal's latitude and generally warm climate. You'll need a full suit on all but the warmest days since a cold offshore current rarely pushes the sea temperature above 18°C (64°F).

It also pays to come with a respectful attitude to the locals. Busy conditions can obviously cause frayed tempers, but keep things cool and you can't fail to enjoy the surf experience on this wave-rich coastline.

Portugal

Spain

Lisbon

Faro

Atlantic
Ocean

Difficulty
Beginner - expert

Hazards
Some quite remote
breaks; possible crowds;
heavy waves; strong rips
and currents on bigger
swells; rocks; dangerous
drivers (the coast road
from Sagres north is
renowned for fatal
accidents)

Season
Year round

Water temperature
15–22°C (59–72°F)

Wetsuit
4/3 steamer and possibly
boots in winter; 3/2
steamer or shortie in
summer

Access
Very variable: good road
access to some breaks,
especially on Algarve
coast; others may be
down long dusty roads or
require a hike

Other local breaks
Spain's Gulf of Cadiz to
the east can be worth
checking for winter swells

While you're there
The Algarve is one of
the premier golfing
destinations in Europe

SOUTHERN PORTUGAL

Proof that quiet waves can still be found in mainland Europe

The strip of surf in Portugal's south-western corner doesn't start in the most auspicious of ways, with the peaks at Cabo de Sines breaking in front of an ugly industrial plant. But things improve rapidly once this fades in your rearview mirror.

And it just gets better the further south you go. Consistent swells roll onto the Atlantic coast year round, where can be found one beach after another with limited access and peaks that are rarely very busy. Once you round Cape St Vincent and hit the Algarve coast, the water warms up noticeably and the bigger Atlantic swells that can often get out of control are cleaned up as they wrap into the tourist beaches around Lagos.

For those looking for solitude, a beach such as Praia de Odeceixe is manna from heaven. Protected from sea breezes by cliffs and located at the end of a dusty minor road a few miles west of the eponymous town, the beach breaks here are never going to be excessively busy.

South of this is one of Portugal's loveliest surf spots, Arrifana. The steep, winding road down to the harbour of this attractive fishing village takes you to an excellent right-hand point break on bigger swells and some fun beach breaks in smaller conditions. And when you're surfed out, you can sit outside the bar above the beach watching the action in the surf and soaking up the evening sun as you sink a cold one. Could it get any better?

The fun continues as you approach Cape St Vincent at Europe's south western tip. Carrapateira is another massive, very consistent beach. If it's too big, you can sidestep it for the smaller, frequently hollow waves around Sagres, although these are usually pretty busy and especially popular with local lid riders who can be pretty territorial.

You're now on to the Algarve coast, which is less consistent than the Atlantic (which has surf year round) and is generally regarded as more of a winter surf zone. The focal point here is Praia da Rocha, which can produce some fun hollow waves but is almost always busy when it's on – and you'll also have to contend with hordes of holidaymakers in and out of the water, turning bright red in the winter sun.

On bigger swells, the more curious may well find surfable beach and point breaks further east towards Faro. It's certainly worth a foray into this surfing backwater, and if you don't score there's still one of Europe's finest winter climates to enjoy along with great local wine and seafood.

Milan
Genova

Italy

*Tyrrhenian
Sea*

Difficulty
Beginner – expert

Hazards
Possible crowds; currents
and rips on bigger swells;
rocks at some breaks; sea
urchins; some spots suffer
from pollution

Season
Year round

Water temperature
13–26°C (55–79°F)

Wetsuit
Steamer and boots
in winter; shortie or
boardshorts in summer

Access
Easy road access to most
main breaks.

Other local breaks
The Italian Adriatic coast
has waves, as does the
French Mediterranean

While you're there
From a cultural point of
view, Italy is probably
number one in the world;
check out the nearby
Leaning Tower of Pisa,
for starters

NORTH WEST ITALY

This unlikely surf zone has it all – when it's on

When considering Italian surf, it's perhaps best to set aside any preconceptions you may have and take a quick look at a map of the Med. Sure, it's a sea rather than an ocean but it can get some ferocious weather, it has a reasonable fetch and Italy is fortunately placed to pick up a lot of the swell that those two phenomena can generate.

Indeed, most of the Italian coastline receives waves at various times, but the focal point of Italian and perhaps Mediterranean surfing is the north-west corner of the country.

Here on beaches, reefs and points either side of Viareggio, there are consistent waves for much of the year, a burgeoning local crew and all the paraphernalia that goes with that, such as surf shops, surf mags and even crowded line ups.

All this has come about because the region can get some really good waves from time to time. The reef at Varazze near Genova, the impressive lefts at Levanto and the beach breaks of Viareggio, when they're firing, are more than enough to make a surf trip to the land of da Vinci and Pavarotti well worthwhile.

As with the rest of Europe, the prime time for waves is winter, when Atlantic lows crossing the mainland or depressions off the North African coast can create fairly consistent swells that are ideal for the 'average' surfer – not too big, not too heavy and lots of fun. However, a full wetsuit will be required.

And that's not to say that more challenging conditions don't occur fairly regularly. Double overhead, barrelling blue walls are more common than you might expect here.

Come the summer months, the surf will drop off and long flat spells are common (although it's not as if there's nothing to do in Italy when the surf doesn't show) but as summer moves into autumn you may catch beautiful conditions – a clean groundswell, offshore breeze and the chance to ride warm Mediterranean waves in nothing more than board shorts.

And it's not just about the surf in Italy. Anyone who has ever skied or boarded in the country will know that the activity you're indulging in is only half the story. The other half is the relaxing over a coffee, a cold beer or a local wine and people-watching, and there's nowhere better to do this than an Italian promenade or beach.

The Mediterranean has virtually no tide so the waves are not tide dependant, which means you can surf when you want and hang out at the beach bar the rest of the time, although swells can be short lived, so don't overdo the café culture. After all, however fascinating the people watching may be, it's always more fun riding waves.

Difficulty
Beginner – expert

Hazards
Possible crowds; currents
and rips on bigger swells;
rocks at some breaks;
sea urchins

Season
Year round

Water temperature
13–24°C (55–75°F)

Wetsuit
Steamer and boots
in winter; shortie or
boardshorts in summer

Access
Good road access to many
of the main breaks

Other local breaks
Corsica to the north and
Sicily to the southeast
both have waves

While you're there
Take a wander around
the attractive old town of
Oristano, close to the best
surf zone; if you're here
in February, check out the
500-year-old equestrian
tournament of Sa Sartiglia
held on Carnival Sunday
and Mardi Gras

SARDINIA, ITALY

Head offshore to discover the Italian island surf scene

It's only in recent years that the quality of Sardinian surf has been recognized, although given the island's location in the middle of the western Mediterranean it should be no real surprise that it receives reasonably consistent surf, especially in winter.

Add to that consistency a decent range of beach, point and reef breaks to suit all abilities, a lovely warm climate for much of the year, friendly locals, great value food, wine and accommodation and what's not to like?

The best surf is on the west coast with a good selection of breaks spread along its length. These pick up waves generated by the north-westerly Mistral wind which blows mainly in winter and spring, although it can occur at other times.

Look for a south or south-west facing stretch of coastline where the wind will be cross/ offshore, such as the area around Chia at the island's southern tip; and when the wind drops off, the whole of the west coast can potentially open up to well developed but short-lived groundswells.

In these conditions, the peninsula west of the coastal village of Putzu Idu is a gathering

point for Sardinian surfers. Here you'll find a lovely, unspoilt coastline with a fine array of breaks, the most popular of which are probably Capo Manu and Mini Capo.

Sparkling turquoise waves that can sometimes reach double overhead barrelling over a rocky sea floor could have you doing a double take – is this really the Med and not the Canaries? Both lefts and rights zip ashore at both breaks, and if these are crowded it's well worth travelling north as you may find quieter waves all the way up as far as the shores of the Golfo dell' Asinara at the island's top end.

The east coast also gets waves, although they're rarely as large and not as consistent, but it may be worth checking out the areas around the south-east and north-east ends of the island for easterly swells rolling in off the Tyrrhenian Sea (which you may well never have heard of).

Sardinia is less than a hundred miles wide so distances between coasts are not great and you should be able to call on the help and advice of the generally friendly locals in your search for surf.

It's also worth asking their advice for the best bars and restaurants. Sardinian food and wine is world class but, when you are spoilt for choice like this, local knowledge is almost as valuable as it is when you are searching out waves.

For European surfers looking for an unusual surf break, Sardinia is worthy of serious consideration. It has surf to suit all abilities and is easily reached by budget airline, which means you should be able to travel at short notice and with luck pick off the best waves in the Med.

Atlantic
Ocean

Spain

Madeira

Morocco

Difficulty
Expert only

Hazards
Big, heavy waves; rocks;
some breaks remote;
currents and rips; some
breaks only accessible via
narrow mountain roads

Season
Winter is prime season

Water temperature
17–22°C (62–72°F)

Wetsuit
3/2 steamer or shortie;
boots useful for rock
hopping

Access
Very variable: good road
access to some breaks,
others may require a hike;
getting in and out of the
surf tricky at most breaks

Other local breaks
None

While you're there
Go hiking along the
agricultural drainage
channels known as
'levadas' for some
spectacular coastal and
mountain views, although
you may need a good
head for heights

MADEIRA ISLAND

Big, spectacular waves that are worth the wait

The hackneyed phrase 'Europe's answer to Hawai'i' has been used for decades to describe one big wave spot after another, but of all of them Madeira has the strongest claim to the title.

And apart from the fact that the water is colder than in Hawai'i, in some ways it could be argued that Madeira is better, for despite regular media exposure the island's world class giant point breaks rarely get anything like as busy.

This is perhaps because there's no history of surf culture here, with the breaks like Jardim do Mar and Paul do Mar on the south–west coast first being surfed less than 20 years ago, while spots such as Ribeira de Janeila on the north coast are even newer discoveries.

What's more, the spectacular coastline of Madeira still holds many more secrets and will probably continue to do so for a long time to come since so much of it is totally inaccessible, fringed by mighty sea cliffs soaring up from deep Atlantic waters and washed by swells that only expert boatmen can expect to negotiate safely.

But Europe's winter surf playground isn't all thundering waves, gentle offshores and sun on your back. It's not uncommon to experience day after day of rain (witness the deluge of February 2010, which caused major flooding and scores of fatalities) along with onshore conditions or flat spells, so a two-week midwinter escape to Madeira will not necessarily guarantee you quality surf.

And there's not much point visiting if your idea of good waves is fun head-high peaks, because it doesn't even start to work properly here until the surf is overhead.

Madeira comes to life when deep low pressure systems in the North Atlantic send north-westerly or west-north-westerly swells marching down to this garden isle in the middle of the ocean. These, combined with offshore north-east trade winds from the African continent, can create the kind of sun-kissed monster walls that very few coastlines in Europe can come close to matching and relatively few surfers have the courage and skill to surf.

For this reason localism is rarely encountered and, indeed, there are still not that many locals in the surf (although the numbers increase annually) since surfing is such a recent introduction. You'll paddle out to join a mixed and eclectic bunch, with surfers from countries as varied as Britain, Norway, Germany and the USA among its numbers.

But you have to be serious about your surfing to join them. Rocky shorelines that make entry and exit tricky at best and big, powerful waves that will challenge the most skilful ensure that Madeira will always be a destination for committed surfers who are not afraid to push themselves and their boards to the limit.

Atlantic
Ocean

Lanzarote

Canary
Islands

Morocco

Difficulty
Beginner – expert

Hazards
Big, heavy waves;
shallow; rocks; sea
urchins; irritating locals

Season
Winter

Water temperature
18 – 22°C (64 – 71°F)

Wetsuit
3/2 steamer or shortie;
boots useful for
rock hopping

Access
Very variable – good road
access to some breaks;
others may be down
rough dirt tracks; getting
in and out of the surf
tricky at many breaks

Other local breaks
The nearby island of
Fuerteventura has a fine
range of breaks

While you're there
Take a tour of Lanzarote's
unforgettable volcanic
landscapes, or head to
the fleshpots of the south
coast for beer, clubs and
general depravity

LANZAROTE, CANARY ISLANDS

Come on in – join the crowds on Lanzarote's north shore

Like the Hawai'ian islands, the Canary Island archipelago of which Lanzarote is part is made from volcanic rocks thrusting up from deep ocean waters. In winter, the swells running into these mini landmasses have usually travelled from intense low pressure systems to the north, so that once they trip over Lanzarote's shallow reefs they burst forward and explode with a power and grace that brings surfers flocking to the island from all over Europe.

It's not all steep, fast reef breaks though. The massive crescent of black sand that is Famara Beach on the north coast also has consistent waves that go from almost flat at one end of the beach to head high-plus at the other end on a good swell, allowing beginners to choose the size they feel most comfortable with and making this probably the most popular novice beach in Europe in winter.

The consistently sunny conditions and warm waters of Lanzarote are another obvious attraction, although this should be tempered with the fact that it's often windy and dusty here; it's a rare surf trip to Lanzarote that doesn't see dust and sand getting everywhere from inside your wettie to your bed.

The action for more experienced wave riders centres on the breaks around La Santa, also on the north coast, where you'll find a selection of left and right hand reef breaks that can work on the biggest of swells and are rarely anything less than fast, hollow and shallow. And they're invariably busy, with aggressive localism a common thing on Lanzarote's north shore.

This is one place where localism seems to have won out, and many visitors simply choose to avoid surfing here as it's just not worth the hassle. The irony of this is that the waves are still busy, even if the majority of the boorish contingent of surfers are locals enjoying a sport that was introduced to the island in the 1970s and 1980s by the kind of people they now regard as personae non gratae.

Indeed, few areas represent the unchilled side of surfing better than Lanzarote's north shore on a busy day, but all is not lost as there are some fine waves to be had on the south-west and north-east coasts and even occasionally around the tourist hot spot of Arrecife for those who would rather avoid the rat pack.

It's unlikely you'll ever score much in the way of real solitude even in these locations, but if you're looking to escape the damp, dark and cold of winter in Europe you may just consider busy waves to be a price worth paying for warm, fast, hollow rides.

ISRAEL

It may not be world class, but a surf trip to Israel is certainly different

Difficulty
Beginner – expert

Hazards
Occasional shallow reef breaks; terrorism

Season
Winter

Water temperature
18–28°C (64–82°F)

Wetsuit
3/2 steamer in winter; boardshorts in summer

Access
Good road access to main breaks although crowded parking spaces can be a problem

Other local breaks
Egypt to the south and Cyprus to the north both get passable surf, especially in winter

While you're there
There are enough cultural and historic sites to keep anyone busy, especially in Jerusalem, or go for a float in the Dead Sea

With around 1,250 miles of fetch, it's not as unlikely as it may seem that Israel has waves along the length of its Mediterranean coastline, although classic days are pretty rare. It's more likely that you'll be riding waist high, onshore mush than anything else. That's not to say that days of clean, overhead barrels don't occur, but even on the bigger days there will be a relative lack of power compared to equivalent sized waves elsewhere.

On the plus side, the water is warm, the sun will usually be shining and there's more often than not the enthusiastic vibe in the water that seems to be characteristic of lesser surf destinations. Israeli surfers are by and large a friendly bunch and seem to enjoy sharing waves. Drop-ins and snaking are common and surfing is a popular summer sport so on the small, choppy days of summer you'll be out there with every form of surf riding craft you can think of, ridden by all ages and both sexes in large numbers.

Not enough to tempt you? If that's the case, consider visiting in winter when the surf is relatively consistent and swells can have enough size to be real fun. The most popular surfing zones are around Tel Aviv, which has a variety of beach breaks and a decent reef in front of the Hilton Hotel – it's always popular, especially with longboarders (that's the reef not the hotel) – and Haifa, where the right-hand reef at Bat Galim or 'Back Door' occasionally puts up a hollow, fast wall and is regarded as the best break in Israel.

However, these two cities also happen to be the largest population centres on the coast, so even in the depths of winter when the water may dip to 18°C (64°F) you'll be sharing the waves with the usual busy and enthusiastic crowd.

Numbers may drop off slightly if you head away from the cities, though, and some of Israel's better waves can be found in the north of the country at spots such as Sokhalov Beach near the Lebanese border.

The mention of Lebanon is likely to bring to mind the tensions that are part and parcel of life in this part of the world and that alone is enough to deter most people from visiting. That's a decision that only the individual can make; for many, the surf would need to be more enticing than it is to overcome this concern. But for those who do take a board to Israel, there's no doubt that it'll be a very different surf experience and also one that is likely to gain you some new friends.

Difficulty
Beginner – expert

Hazards
Intense sun in summer;
possible culture clashes
with the authorities;
jellyfish swarms in winter

Season
Winter

Water temperature
14–27°C (57–80°F)

Wetsuit
4/3 steamer in winter,
shortie or boardshorts
rest of the year

Access
Road access varies from
smooth blacktop to
bumpy and potholed

Other local breaks
Morocco's Atlantic coast is
the best bet for consistent
waves in North Africa

While you're there
Explore the cities and
culture of the Arab world
or take a snowboard and
go sand surfing at the Sea
of Sands near Alexandria

NORTH AFRICA'S MEDITERRANEAN COAST

A curious place to surf

The Mediterranean shores of France, Italy and Sardinia have seen surfing take off markedly in recent years, and it doesn't take a genius to realise that those countries on the opposite side of the Med must also pick up swells from the not infrequent storms and depressions that hit this inland sea. Indeed, more intrepid surf explorers from France and Italy have been travelling to North Africa's Mediterranean shores from time to time in recent years to pick off some quality waves in glorious solitude.

Algeria, Tunisia, Libya and western Egypt are all exposed to sufficient fetch to see occasional well lined up and quite acceptable swells hit their shores.

But it is rare for many of the breaks in these Arab nations to be ridden regularly, despite the increasing number of French and Italian surfers exploring here in the winter. (That said, there are a few locals in Alexandria.)

So, if you have the freedom and the money to study weather charts and head to North Africa when things are looking up, you have a very, very good chance of getting the surf to yourself.

Winter is prime time, when depressions may move through the Med and result in either localized wind swells or short lived ground swells, while winds such as the north-westerly Mistral over southern Europe can blow long and hard enough to send a well organized swell onto the beaches, coves and points of the southern Mediterranean shores − goofies will find a wealth of lefts, especially along Tunisia's northern shores.

For sure, you're not going to discover Pacific power and size, but waist high to overhead waves are not uncommon in winter and even in summer, when boardshorts and sunscreen are the go, lazy windswells can make a visit to the beach eminently worthwhile.

Assuming you can find anyone to surf with, it's likely to be an expat who is working in the region and has had the nous to bring a board along for their overseas sojourn, as any surfer worthy of the name should.

As far as locals are concerned, well, to all intents and purposes there are none; your wave riding activities are likely to elicit various responses from bemusement to amusement, although the authorities can't be relied upon not to take an unwelcome interest too, so, as always when travelling, treading lightly and respecting local cultures are essential attributes.

It would be easy to imagine there could be a clash between the Western culture of board riders and the traditional lifestyle of the local population. However, few surfers who have ridden the waves of, say, Algeria and Tunisia have met with anything other than friendliness and warmth from the residents they've met on their wave hunts. (Maybe if politicians were required to undertake a two week surfari every year the world would be a better place.)

Spain

*Atlantic
Ocean*

Morocco

Algeria

Mauritania

Difficulty
Beginner – expert

Hazards
Some shallow, rocky
breaks; sea urchins; touts
and thieves

Season
Winter is prime season

Water temperature
16–22°C (60–72°F)

Wetsuit
3/2 steamer in winter;
shortie or boardshorts in
summer

Access
Good road access to
main breaks

Other local breaks
The entire Atlantic
coastline of Morocco has
great wave potential

While you're there
If time permits, consider
a trip to the nearby Atlas
Mountains for great
views and great hiking,
mountain biking and
maybe even skiing

MOROCCO

Regular foot desert paradise

If your idea of a great time is surfing long, walling right handers feathering in an
offshore breeze, then the area of Central Morocco focusing on Agadir is definitely one to
put on your tick list.

The coastline to the north of Agadir faces south-west and is ideally placed to pick
up winter north-westerly swells that wrap in to produce a fine selection of point breaks.
The icing on the cake are the north-easterly trade winds, which blow pretty consistently
throughout this period to hold up the wave faces and allow you to speed down the
line and tuck into the barrel at top quality locales such as Killer Point and the classic
Anchor Point.

The latter is the break that appears so often in images of Moroccan surf, and it's a
great introduction to more serious waves for intermediate surfers, although its quality and
fame can often mean it's pretty busy.

Not to worry, though; there are plenty of other options if it's looking crowded in the
lineup at Anchor's. An easy introduction to the area, and readily accessible just to the

north of Agadir, are the river mouth at Banana Beach and the beach breaks at Tamghart. Relatively gentle waves roll ashore here over a sandy sea floor (hence the surf school students you'll probably encounter) and provide a fun rather than challenging ride.

All the better point breaks are easily reached to the north and, although they can get quite busy, on a good day the waves are so consistent and the rides so long that they can generally handle the crowds. The great thing about this area is that there are quality point breaks to suit just about every level of surfer. Few would disagree that Anchor Point on a big swell is world class, for instance, but if you're after something less challenging than that, the attractive beach at Immesouane further north has more mellow rights on smaller swells.

Should the surf go flat, you're unlikely to get bored if you take the opportunity to explore a little. A trip to Marrakesh is always favourite for the chance to immerse yourself in Islamic culture and architecture, and get cheerfully ripped off in one of the souks. That said, you may find that the non-stop hassle from touts can wear thin pretty quickly and it is undoubtedly a problem when travelling in Morocco.

If you really want to escape the touts – and other surfers – get yourself a four-wheel drive and plenty of supplies, and head south from Agadir. It won't be long before you're driving along empty roads with the Atlantic on one side, the Sahara on the other and literally thousands of miles of wave washed coastline ahead of you, where you'll have no trouble whatsoever in finding the perfect beach or point break to share with your mates.

Atlantic Ocean

● **Mauritania**

Senegal

Mali

Difficulty
Strong intermediate – expert

Hazards
Remote; sunburn, dust and dehydration; some shallow breaks

Season
Year round but winter most consistent

Water temperature
18–24°C (64–75°F)

Wetsuit
3/2 steamer or shortie

Access
Difficult

Other local breaks
Senegal to the south has some good quality and much more accessible waves

While you're there
Relax and read a good book – there's very little else to occupy you

MAURITANIA, WEST AFRICA

Empty waves guaranteed between the desert and the ocean

Mauritania isn't quite off the radar in surfing terms, but it's pretty low on it. Ever since exotic shots of waves breaking off the rusted hulk of a beached freighter on one of the country's deserted Atlantic beaches appeared in surf magazines in the '70s, this relatively unknown desert nation has held a special place on the list of 'must surf' destinations for adventurous surf travellers.

But the fact that almost 40 years down the line very few people have ticked Mauritania off their list shows how remote and inaccessible the country's waves are. Few roads access any part of Mauritania, and while the coastal road that takes you past the country's endless beaches is in relatively good repair and regularly used, you still need a fully kitted out four-wheel drive and a driver who knows how to handle it to ensure safe travel, since you have the mighty expanse of the Sahara on one side and the equally mighty expanse of the Atlantic on the other – that's around 3,000 miles of wilderness to both east and west.

This is the kind of place where you'll find no named breaks and no directions. Exploration is very much the key, but you need to temper that with caution. Note, for instance, that there are said to be unexploded land mines in some parts of the country from previous altercations between former colonial powers, so venturing off the beaten track should be undertaken with caution.

The waves that pound Mauritania's coastline emanate primarily from North Atlantic depressions, with winter being the most consistent season, when you'll find clean, crisp beach, point and reef breaks with a chill offshore wind from the desert fanning their faces.

It's not often that you'd curse an offshore wind as a surfer, but this particular wind can be a nuisance at times. If it gets up any strength, as can frequently happen, it will also be carrying a hefty load of the Sahara with it, which will end up in your eyes, your mouth, your hair and inside wetsuits, tents and cars, making life a bit gritty in every sense of the word.

Even though you're in one of the driest and hottest places in Africa you'll probably need to wear a wettie of some sort, the more so because the sea isn't as warm here as the proximity of the very tropical Senegal and Gambia to the south might suggest.

Indeed, these two surf rich nations are likely to also be on your itinerary if you're surfing in Mauritania, since it's not the kind of place you fly into for a couple of weeks of relaxed surfing. Most travellers, in fact, will probably have travelled south from Morocco and Western Sahara – one hell of surf trip, and one where Mauritania is likely to be a highlight.

●Namibia

Botswana

Atlantic
Ocean

South Africa

Difficulty
Expert

Hazards
Shallow, rocky breaks;
heavy waves; remote;
seals and sharks;
harsh climate

Season
Year round

Water temperature
13–20°C (55–68°F)

Wetsuit
4/3 or 3/2 steamer;
shortie possible in
summer; boots useful for
accessing reefs

Access
Good road access to
most named breaks;
others may be very
difficult to access

Other local breaks
The entire Atlantic
coastline of Namibia has
great wave potential, as
does that of South Africa
to the south

While you're there
Extend your exploration
by driving up to the
Skeleton Coast (named
after the numerous
shipwrecks you'll find)
where there's equally
good surf to be had – but
lots of sharp-toothed
wildlife to share it with

NAMIBIA
Wild surfing for the wild at heart

Namibia isn't the kind of place you surf on a whim. Whichever section of its 900-mile long coastline you choose to surf, you'll essentially have the vast, shifting sands of the Namib Desert on one side and the cold, deep blue waters of the Atlantic on the other. And very little else. You'll also be sharing the waves with seals and sharks, both of which have been known to take lumps out of surfers...

On the plus side, if you're self-sufficient and enjoy exploring wild landscapes and riding wild surf, a surfari through Namibia is an unforgettable experience. Probably the best base along the coast is the popular tourist town of Swakopmund, which you can either fly into or drive to, but it's almost 1,250 miles from Cape Town to the south so plan on at least two days for this particular approach (and more if you stop off and get a few waves en route).

Indeed, if you drive you'll likely find as many good waves along the way as you will around Swakopmund, but the advantage of using the town as a base is that you have all the luxuries of twenty-first century living whilst easily being able to venture into wild terrain to north and south.

Plus, there are plenty of named surf spots in the area that are easy to find. These are invariably pretty serious breaks, often shallow, fast and heavy. Examples include Lockjoint and Tiger Reef in the town, the left hand point break of Paradise to the south of town and the reef break of Fiji to the north of town, perhaps the most user-friendly wave in the area.

The name of the latter break is misleading, however. Namibia's coastline is about as far removed from Fiji's as you can get, and this is what makes surfing here a serious proposition.

Once you're away from coastal settlements the landscape is harsh and arid and the climate borders on the bizarre; inland, hot days of up to 35°C (95°F) may be followed by nights when it gets as cold as freezing and, while it's generally less extreme along the coast, you have constant fog to deal with for as many as 340 days per year.

This is caused by the cold Benguela Current offshore, which also makes the water far colder than you might expect at this latitude (the same as that of southern Madagascar).

And although there's the potential to discover endless new breaks, you may only be able to access them along rough dirt tracks through sand dunes – not the kind of place you want to have a puncture or get stuck.

On the plus side there are very few flat days, especially in winter, most breaks remain relatively uncrowded and this is a place where you can still sense the adventure of surf exploration even though others may have gone before you.

South Africa

Cape Town

St Francis Bay

Difficulty
Beginner – expert

Hazards
Sharks; some shallow
breaks; sharp, mussel
covered rocks

Season
Year round

Water temperature
15 – 21°C (59 – 69°F)

Wetsuit
4/3 or 3/2 steamer;
shortie possible in
summer; boots useful for
crossing rocks

Access
Good road access
to most breaks

Other local breaks
The Wild Coast to the
north offers plenty of
opportunities to discover
quiet, quality waves

While you're there
There's not a great deal
to do locally other than
surf but car hire is cheap
and will let you access
everything from the
Garden Route coastal
drive to the Drakensberg
Mountains

ST FRANCIS BAY,
SOUTH AFRICA

The legendary endless waves
of Endless Summer

Almost 50 years ago, Bruce Brown 'chanced across' St Francis Bay while filming
everyone's favourite wet Sunday afternoon surf film Endless Summer, and no one who has
seen the movie can fail to imagine what it must have been like to share the endless right
hand point break that he captured on film with just a couple of mates.

That is not a scenario that is ever likely to happen again since the intervening decades
have seen generations of surfers descend on St Francis Bay, not just to surf 'Bruce's
Beauties' but also to catch the far superior waves just up the coast at Jeffrey's Bay.

Quite rightly 'J-Bay' is regarded as one of the finest right hand point breaks on the
planet, which on a big south or south-west swell can connect up as many as seven
sections to give a phenomenally long ride of superb quality. The walls seem to go on
forever, throwing out into one barrelling section after the next, which will see you shacked
as well as worn out by the end of the ride.

If these two waves were all that St Francis Bay had to offer most people would be happy, but far from it – there's a selection of lefts, rights and beach breaks all the way from the sharky Seal Point at the bay's western tip to Cape Recife near the city of Port Elizabeth, some 100 km away at the eastern end of the bay.

This means the surf pilgrims who flock to the focal point of Jeffrey's Bay have plenty to share out amongst themselves, which is a good thing since a surf zone this good will always be busy.

Winter is the best time to visit, when swells pour up from the Roaring Forties to the south and it's rare to have flat spells. Since this also coincides with the flattest surf season in Europe, it's no surprise to find plenty of European surfers visiting at this time of year, along with the healthy population of locals and visitors from all parts of the globe who came and never left.

This lends a fairly cosmopolitan atmosphere to the scene although it does mean there will always be a lot of very good wave riders in the water when it's on, so patience and respect are necessary to ensure everyone rubs along together.

A healthy respect is also necessary for the local shark population. Although shark attacks on surfers are inevitably blown up out of all proportion by the media, you'd be a fool to dismiss the very negligible but still real threat of sharks here, and it makes sense to keep out of the water in twilight, after heavy rainfall or during the annual sardine run in June and July.

The chances are, however, that your biggest worry will be aching legs and salt stung eyes from long hours of surfing some of the best rights you're ever likely to score.

Western
Australia

Australia

Batavia
Coast

Indian Ocean

Difficulty
Expert

Hazards
Big, powerful swells;
sharks; sharp, shallow
reefs; isolation; harsh
desert conditions; snakes
and scorpions

Season
Winter

Water temperature
18–21°C (64–70°F)

Wetsuit
3/2 steamer or shortie;
boots useful for avoiding
reef cuts

Access
Decent road access to
better known breaks;
more remote spots
will require four-wheel
drive and the skills to
handle it properly

Other local breaks
You're in Western
Australia – there
are quality waves
everywhere!

While you're there
Continue north to
Monkey Mia – not only
will you find more surf
but you can also swim
with the wild dolphins at
the famous reserve

BATAVIA COAST, WESTERN AUSTRALIA

Serious waves for serious surfers

Western Australia is a region the size of Western Europe with enough world class surf to last you a lifetime, so let's narrow it down a tad and focus on the relatively small stretch of coast between Geraldton and Kalbarri. This will provide you with as hardcore an adventure as most surfers are ever likely to find in an English-speaking country.

The best way of exploring this coast is to drive up from Perth, ideally in a four-wheel drive, which will need to be well equipped for desert conditions if you're planning to get serious about your surf exploration.

There are plenty of surf spots en route but assuming you gun it to the crayfishing capital of Geraldton, once you paddle out you'll find you're joining a no-nonsense resident surf population who have the local breaks such as the peaks of Back Beach or the more serious offshore reef of Hell's Gate well wired.

The same really applies to everywhere you'll be surfing in this part of the world. Those who surf here are serious about their surfing, since you don't really want to be paddling out to the shallow, sharp and powerful reefs that are encountered almost everywhere in this rugged corner of Western Australia if you don't know what you're doing.

In addition, many of the better reefs are a mile or so offshore – not the place to be getting into trouble. And needless to say, several species of shark frequent the waters; bounce off a reef and leave a trail of blood in the water and you never know who might sniff it out.

On top of all of this is the remoteness of many of the breaks. While Geraldton and Kalbarri have their fair share of waves, most of the breaks along the 60 mile stretch in between will be booming ashore in glorious isolation and may only be accessible down a baking hot, dusty, washboard dirt road where the only 'facilities' of any sort will be those you carry with you.

To make the most of the area, you should visit in winter when the southerly swells that create the surf are incredibly consistent and will rarely drop below head high. This also gives you the advantage of travelling in cooler weather as well as missing the windy conditions that are a feature of the hotter months and can mess up any swell for days at a time.

As with much of the rest of Western Australia's coastline, the waves along the Batavia Coast don't go out of their way to be friendly but if you want adventure and challenge they'll provide that in abundance.

TEMPERATE

Western Australia
Australia
● **Perth**

Indian Ocean

Difficulty
Beginner – expert

Hazards
Shallow reefs and
fast heavy waves;
sharks; crowds

Season
Winter can be big but out
of control, especially on
Rottnest; summer will be
much smaller but usually
cleaner

Water temperature
16–22°C (60–72°F)

Wetsuit
3/2 steamer in winter;
shortie or boardshorts
and rash vest in summer;
boots useful for reefs

Access
Most breaks easily
accessed by road apart
from a few reef breaks
around Lancelin that
require a boat

Other local breaks
Continue south to
Margaret River for big,
world class surf

While you're there
Perth and Fremantle are
great bases for partying
and meeting fellow
travellers; Rottnest is a
great base for meeting
quokkas, friendly little
marsupials (don't feed
them though) or spotting
humpback whales
migrating north

PERTH, WESTERN AUSTRALIA

Better than it seems at first sight

Before all those who have surfed the generally small and uninspiring waves of Perth rise up in revolt at its inclusion here, let's point out that we're looking at Perth as little more than a base for exploring the infinitely better waves of Rottnest Island, and Lancelin and Mandurah to the north and south respectively.

So, while Perth is unlikely to float your boat as far as the waves are concerned, apart from phenomenally crowded Triggs Point (Cable Station artificial reef in Cottesloe, constructed in 2000, simply proves that nature does a much better job of making surf breaks), this is a great city in which to spend some time if you're travelling around Oz. Make forays out from the metropolitan area to hit the region's better waves, all of which are within an hour or two's drive or a short ferry journey.

Lancelin is just 80 miles north of Perth on a good coastal road and has a selection of beach breaks and quality right hand reef breaks that pick up plenty of swell and make the short drive well worthwhile.

Even closer is Mandurah, an attractive and increasingly popular tourist town around 40 miles south of Perth, which has a good variety of waves. Mandurah will be more appealing

to less accomplished surfers, who will enjoy the fun beach breaks at Blue Bay and Falcon Bay; better wave riders can take on various left hand reef breaks such as Miami Reef and Melrose.

Even closer – within eyesight of Perth's busy beaches, in fact – is Rottnest Island, a few miles offshore. In large part, this is the culprit behind the city's poor quality surf since it blocks much of the swell that would otherwise hit the metropolitan beaches. A tiny knee-high swell on the Perth beaches will probably be head high out on Rottnest (and a similar size in Lancelin and Mandurah). This is the cue to take the half-hour ferry ride out to the island after which you'll have to hire a bike to get to the breaks, since only residents are allowed to use cars on Rottnest's roads.

The island's blinding white sand beaches slip away into the kind of aquamarine waters that are more often associated with Western Australia's more northerly coastline, and off these you'll find waves that are a world away from the crowded mush in Perth.

For sure there will be plenty of other surfers all over it on a good swell, but nothing like the masses on the mainland. On a good swell, if you catch breaks like the popular Strickland Bay or the bigger wave spots of Cathedrals and Radar Reef, next door to each other at the southwest tip of the island, you'll pat yourself on the back for taking the time and effort to get out here.

What's more, when you get back to Perth you can enjoy the benefits of a night out in one of Australia's finest and most attractive cities, thus proving there is plenty to be said for 'surfing' in Perth.

Australia

Victoria

Melbourne

Indian Ocean

Difficulty
Beginner – expert

Hazards
Big powerful swells
common and can pick
up quickly at times;
some shallow breaks;
rips and currents

Season
Year round

Water temperature
13–19°C (55–66°F)

Wetsuit
4/3 or 3/2 steamer;
boots useful in winter
and at rocky breaks

Access
Good road access to
most breaks

Other local breaks
The beach breaks at
Johanna to the west of
Cape Otway are a good
option on smaller days

While you're there
Visit the excellent
Surfworld surf museum
in Torquay; check out the
famous Twelve Apostles
sea stacks along the
Great Ocean Road

VICTORIA, AUSTRALIA

Great waves for everyone in the 'Garden State'

The focal point of surfing in Victoria is along the scenic Great Ocean Road, which in
the 60 or so miles between Cape Otway and the state's surf capital of Torquay takes you
past a treasure trove of beach, point and river mouth breaks, including one of the finest
rights in Australia at Bell's Beach, which hosts the world's longest running surf contest
each year.

That such quality surf is to be found here is no real surprise since the mighty swells
generated in the Southern Ocean come crashing into the temperate green shores of
Victoria with nothing to stop them (well, nothing other than Tasmania, which blocks
south-east swells – but that still leaves more than enough surf).

Add predominantly offshore winds and a mellow climate without the temperature
extremes of many other parts of Australia and it all makes for a world class surf
playground. Sure, you'll need to wear a wettie year-round and winters are a bit on the
cool side, but these are minor inconveniences.

The importance of the art of wave riding to this region is not to be underestimated. Two or three generations of the same family may be found together out in the surf at spots such as Anglesea and Lorne, and the region boasts the world's first Surfing Recreation Reserve, at Bells Beach. This was designated an ' *International Icon of Australian surfing culture*' almost 40 years ago – a pity more surf communities around the world don't show such enlightened attitudes to the sport.

Of course, the downside of all this is that you're never likely to get an especially quiet session in the waves and even on smaller days you'll be competing hard to get set waves since everyone and his dog surfs – and surfs well – around here.

But with the wealth of breaks to choose from, you can at least play to your own strengths. Want a febrile session with the best around? The rights of Bells or Winkipop on a clean overhead swell will provide that in bucketloads. Want a more relaxed session where fun rather than competition is the goal? Check out the breaks at Kennet River or nearby Wye River. Looking for an easily accessed beach break for all the family? Try 13th Beach at Barwon Heads.

This is easy territory in which to be a surfer, too; with plenty of cheap accommodation and a surf-savvy population, you'll fit in like a local with a board on the roof and a wettie on your back.

In fact, you may find you end up becoming a local. Plenty of visitors have come to ride the waves along the Great Ocean Road and ended up staying.

Canada

Vancouver **Christina Lake**

USA

Difficulty
Intermediate

Hazards
Engine fumes

Season
Summer

Water temperature
18–23°C (64–73°F)

Wetsuit
Shortie or boardshorts

Access
Good road access
and boat ramps at
several beaches

Other local breaks
The nearest waves are
two days drive away
on the Pacific coast

While you're there
The hiking and mountain
biking locally are
exceptional; nearby
Rossland has some of
the most challenging
mountain bike trails in
British Columbia

CHRISTINA LAKE, BRITISH COLUMBIA

Warm water and inland waves – as long as you have a powerful boat

The tranquil blue water of a Canadian lake, lined by fir trees and surrounded by majestic mountains, is not the kind of place you'd expect to be enjoying what could be the longest wave of your life, but surfers are nothing if not resourceful, and the wave starved dudes of southern British Columbia have come up with the next best thing to real surf in the heart of hike, bike and ski country.

Here's how it works: you get yourself a powerful boat, fill it with buddies, beer and ballast, attach a tow rope and throw in your board of choice. Head out onto the lake, rev her up, and you can end up with a wake that's shoulder high.

Drop into this via the tow rope (or once you've got it wired just hop over the side of the boat and straight onto your board) and it's possible to 'surf' for 10 minutes or more – or until your legs give up on you.

And just as bizarre as the fact that you're surfing surrounded by lumberjack landscapes is the fact that in midsummer you can do so in nothing more than boardies. Christina Lake is the warmest lake in BC, with water temperatures rising as high as 23°C (73°F) in July and August.

Combine this with the region's delightful summer climate of long, warm sunny days in the mid to high 20s Celsius (70s–80s Fahrenheit) and Canadian surfing takes on a whole new dimension, far removed from the frigid water of Nova Scotia or Vancouver Island.

The lake has a number of beaches around its shores, with boat access at several, so hook up with the right locals and you could find yourself riding waves several hundred miles from the nearest ocean.

Of course, this is a pretty costly way of surfing (and one that will have the eco warriors up in arms) so you won't be out on the water all day, but with 10-minute rides you don't need to be. As Jim Greene, one of the pioneers of the Christina Lake surf scene points out, 'I can catch one wave and ride as long as I would in two weeks surfing down in Mexico!'

And while the manoeuvres you can perform on a wake wave are limited, it's not quite as easy as it sounds. You'll find that fresh water has less buoyancy than salt water so you may require a bigger board than you're used to, the more so since the waves have less power than a regular ocean wave.

But on the plus side, if you swallow a mouthful of water when you wipe out, it's a lot more palatable than sea water!

Virginia

North
Carolina **Outer Banks**

North
Atlantic
Ocean

Difficulty
Beginner – expert

Hazards
Cold water in winter;
rips and currents

Season
Year round

Water temperature
6–25°C (42–77°F)

Wetsuit
Full winter steamer,
boots and gloves right
through to boardshorts
and rash vest

Access
Good road access

Other local breaks
Ocrakoke Island to the
south-west has miles of
beach breaks

While you're there
Check out the Wright
Brothers Museum in Kitty
Hawk – the first guys in
the world to see lines of
swell from the air

OUTER BANKS, NORTH CAROLINA

From frigid to subtropical in a matter of weeks

Few places in the world have such a huge variation in water temperature as the Outer Banks, from a digit numbing 6°C (42°F) in winter to a supremely pleasant 25°C (77°F) in summer.

Unfortunately, as is so often the case, the biggest and most consistent surf usually rolls in when the weather is coldest, from November through to March, but late summer and autumn can offer great conditions when the water is balmy if not outright warm.

Primo conditions are usually provided by north-east ground swells or courtesy of the hurricanes, which track (ideally) well offshore and send powerful, lined up swells marching onto the sandbanks to create perfect barrels if you're lucky. And when the waves start to close out, as may happen if the swell gets too big, the various piers along the coast such as Kitty Hawk and Avalon can slap the swell into shape and give clean, rideable, overhead surf.

Although the Outer Banks' waves are popular, especially at holiday periods and weekends, and there's a healthy local contingent picking off the best peaks around the piers, there are miles of empty, open beaches somewhat reminiscent of France's Les Landes region where you should be able to access your own peak. If you have a four-wheel drive, you won't even need to walk far since there are vehicle access points at intervals along the coast. (Indeed, Les Landes also gets its best surf at the same time of year and from the same hurricanes that are feeding the Outer Banks.)

There are several specific surf spots. Rodanthe Pier, for instance, is the most exposed location on a very exposed coastline and picks up as much swell as anywhere, but you'll be vying with a competitive local crew to get shacked here. The town of Waves gives you a pretty clear idea of what you may find by its beachfront real estate, and on a southerly swell Frisco Pier is a pretty sure fire spot.

The exposure of the Outer Banks, which sit in splendid isolation off the mainland coast of North Carolina, means they're prone to shifting sand banks and strong longshore drift, so waves will come and go as storms and swells move the sand around and only the piers remain consistent (and even here sea floor conditions – and thus the waves – can vary markedly).

The longshore drift can also mean constant paddling to stay in the lineup on bigger swells, but when the sun is shining, the water is in the 20s Celsius (70s Fahrenheit) and overhead barrels are offering themselves up for your pleasure, who minds a little hard work?

San Francisco

California

Orange County

North Pacific Ocean

Difficulty
Beginner – expert

Hazards
Crowds and frayed tempers

Season
Year round

Water temperature
14–19°C (57–66°F)

Wetsuit
3/2 steamer; shortie possible in summer; boardshorts feasible on warm summer days and smaller swells

Access
Good road access to many breaks but parking can be a problem

Other local breaks
To the north are the legendary point breaks of Malibu, while to the south is San Diego and its quality reef, point and beach breaks

While you're there
Take a wander around Huntington's surf shops, surf museum, surf bars, surf hostels, surf cafes – surf everything; or hit Hollywood or crazy Venice Beach in LA

ORANGE COUNTY, CALIFORNIA

Immerse yourself in surf culture, hype and some great waves

In many respects, Orange County is the home of modern surfing in the same way that nearby Hollywood is the home of movies. Neither is the birthplace of its defining activity but each has taken it to their heart and fostered what many would agree is a bit of a bastard child.

Consistent waves and a superb climate are the understandable attraction for any surfer coming to Orange County, but the hype and over-commercialization that are a fundamental part of Southern Californian living can be hard to deal with at times.

Still, if you have any feeling for or interest in surf culture it's hard to resist a visit to the home turf of US surfing and, as far as waves are concerned, well, here's a sample of what you get in a mere 40-mile stretch of coastline.

Heading north from the super mellow longboard waves of San Onofre, you come to the ultra-competitive high performance rights of Upper and Lower Trestles (to be technically correct, those three waves are actually in San Diego County). Continuing on past San Clemente, home of pretty average beach and pier breaks and the far from average Surfrider Foundation, you come to Salt Creek with its varied selection of top quality breaks, then chic Laguna Beach's fun peaks. Onwards to Corona del Mar's jetty and past bodyboarder's limb snapper The Wedge, you reach 'surf city' Huntington with plenty of waves and plenty of surfers riding them. (It was here that Irish-Hawai'ian surfer and lifeguard George Freeth introduced surfing to the USA in the early 1900s).

Not only has every surfer heard of all these spots, they'll also have seen the waves glittering in soft Southern California evening sunlight in magazines and movies, their faces being carved apart by any one of a score or more of world class surfers who were born and raised here – and that comment could have applied as much 50 years ago as it does today.

Everyone seems to surf in Orange County and unless you're out of bed before daybreak there's very little chance of getting a wave to yourself. The best way of dealing with this is to head for the less accessible spots such as Cottons, or simply grin and bear it. This being California, you'll probably do a lot of grinning anyway, at the regular assortment of wackos of all ages and both sexes riding every form of surf craft ever invented.

Stick it out, though, and you're bound to catch a few good waves for yourself. And as you take off on a shimmering head-high left at Salt Creek and race towards shore with the sun warm on your back and a gentle offshore caressing your cheeks, you'll know, however briefly, why people have been so surf obsessed in Orange County for more than a century.

San
Francisco

California

North Pacific
Ocean

San Diego

Difficulty
Beginner – expert

Hazards
Crowds; localism; urchins
at some rocky breaks

Season
Year round

Water temperature
14–20°C (57–68°F)

Wetsuit
3/2mm steamer in winter;
summer steamer or
shortie in summer;
boots useful for reef and
urchin protection

Access
Easy

Other local breaks
Pop over the border to
Mexico for more waves
and fewer surfers

While you're there
Check out the California
Surf Museum in Oceanside
to the north

LA JOLLA, SAN DIEGO, CALIFORNIA

The essential California surf experience

Trying to choose the best surf spots in Southern California is a bit like trying to decide between a Porsche, a Ferrari and an Aston Martin – there's too much of a good thing to be able to think straight.

But if any area south of LA could be said to epitomize the Southern California surf experience it's probably La Jolla (pronounced 'La Hoya'), a bump of real estate north of San Diego that rolls out into the Pacific like a beer belly and not only has every kind of wave you could ever want breaking on its shores but also has the loveliest coastline in the region.

This is another one of those surf areas that has been so well documented in magazines and movies over the last 50 years that there's a strange familiarity when you first arrive on La Jolla's shore, even if you've never visited before.

Wander down to the swell magnet of Black's Beach with its three distinct peaks, all remarkably heavy for a beach break. Paddle out among the university students at Scripps Pier, bunking out of school and crowding out the break; take on the challenge of La Jolla Cove, one of Southern California's best big wave spots; or catch a few at one of California's most famous breaks, the delightfully named Windansea, which always seems to be bigger than everywhere else in summer.

Chances are you'll have heard of all of these breaks and, in many ways, to surf here is to pay homage to generations of surfers who came before you, many of who have literally shaped the way we surf today. One local break, for instance, is called Simmons, a fast, shallow winter wave named after legendary board designer Bob Simmons who drowned here in 1954.

It goes without saying that in this part of the world being a surfer is as much a part of life as going to school or work. In fact, for many it's more a part of life than school or work, so lineups will always be busy, the standard of wave riding will be very high and you'll have to work to catch your waves.

Winter tends to be quieter and, of course, has bigger and more consistent waves. And for surfers from colder climes, what the locals consider to be a chilly day will invariably seem balmy and pretty user friendly.

But late summer is really the time to visit for the quintessential California surf experience, when the sun shines brightly, the ocean is warmly welcoming and the beach is quite simply the only place to be.

Ecuador

Chicama

Peru

Bolivia

Pacific
Ocean

Difficulty
Intermediate – expert

Hazards
Rips and currents;
leg fatigue

Season
Year round

Water temperature
17–21°C (62–70°F)

Wetsuit
3/2 steamer; shortie in
summer; boots useful
for rock hopping and
long walks

Access
Good road access but
long journey there

Other local breaks
There are more excellent
lefts both north and south
of Chicama

While you're there
Take a good book or
two – there's really very
little else in the way of
amusement unless you're
staying at the surf camp

CHICAMA, PERU

Long and relentless – and that's just the walk back to the take off point

You need strong quads to surf Chicama, not just because this amazing left is one of the world's longest ocean waves with rides of several hundred yards par for the course, but because after each ride you'll also have a lot of walking to do to get back to the take off point.

Yes, you could paddle back out, but a six hundred yard paddle for each wave? Maybe not...

Chicama is so long that you don't even need to make your way out to the outside take off point; you can pick it up at pretty much any point as the wave peels inexorably shorewards and get a ride that will be long enough to keep anyone satisfied.

Oh, and the winds are almost permanently offshore.

What's more, it's not even an especially challenging wave unless it's really big. It rolls rather than barrels, so you're not racing to keep ahead of the lip; it breaks over a mix of sand and rocks rather than some hideous razor sharp reef; and it's rarely exceptionally crowded, despite the quality of the wave (although there's now a surf camp in Chicama so the break isn't quite the remote outpost of South American surfing that it once was).

Even so, unlike so many of the planet's other world class waves, you don't need to be Mr Hot from Hotville to have a cooking session at Chicama.

Chicama Point itself is about two and a half miles long and the wave that breaks along its length has three distinct sections: Malpaso, which breaks for about 150 yards, Keys, at about 600 yards long, and Main Point, which as the name suggest is what everybody makes the fuss about.

The three sections don't connect, but on an overhead swell Main Point will link up with two other inside sections to give a possible ride of one and a half miles. Few people bother to surf it this far, possibly because they get too tired, and they certainly don't want to paddle or walk that far back for their next wave.

And think about it – a one and a half mile ride will take you around four minutes, which is way more time than most of us spend up and riding on an entire session, let alone one wave. So will your legs even take it?

Incredibly, 25 miles distant there's an even longer left called Pacasmayo, which is more consistent, bigger and faster than Chicama. So, should you ever get bored of 'the world's longest left', you can go and surf a longer and better one just up the coast.

The only down side to spending a week or two in Chicama is that it's actually quite a dull spot, and it takes quite a bit of getting to. The coastal landscape is a uniform drab browny–grey and even the sea doesn't glitter turquoise and green as it should in perfect surf pics. Perhaps that just goes to show that even the 'perfect' wave is never quite perfect.

Difficulty
Expert

Hazards
Big, heavy waves;
shallow; rocky; sea urchins

Season
Year round but
autumn/winter biggest
and most consistent

Water temperature
16–20°C (60–68°F)

Wetsuit
3/2mm steamer in winter;
summer steamer or
shortie in summer;
boots useful for reef and
urchin protection

Access
Easy

Other local breaks
The coastline either side
of Iquique has plenty
of world class surf,
although you may need a
four-wheel drive to access
some breaks

While you're there
Take a trip into the
Atacama Desert, which
despite being the
world's driest desert
is surprisingly green
in places

IQUIQUE, CHILE

Big, powerful and incredibly consistent, but not for novices

With its vast coastline it seems unfair to pick out just two surf zones in Chile (also see p200), but very few surfers will ever have the time to explore this long sliver of a country in any real depth, so your best bet is to focus on a particular area – and Iquique is one of the best, as long as you like challenges.

The city, set between the Pacific and the bone dry Atacama Desert, has a very fine selection of easily accessible but extremely challenging reef breaks that are within walking distance of the city centre and each other. This has obvious advantages if you're travelling on a tight budget since you don't need a car to get to the waves.

It also creates a rather strange mix of urban life sitting cheek by jowl with the raw power of the Pacific Ocean. For make no mistake, the waves that crack across Iquique's reefs are pretty much without exception big, powerful and not prone to suffering fools gladly.

They roll ashore from deep water after having been generated by the endless storms of the Roaring Forties way down south. By the time they've crossed the 20° of latitude to Iquique's shoreline these swells are lined up like well drilled soldiers and have lost little of the power they were born with, breaking onto shallow, urchin infested rocks at spots such as (from north to south) Colegio, Punta Dos and Punta Una, to name but three breaks within sight of each other.

All of these spots are rights, and will see thundering barrels sucking almost dry and racing across the shallows to give a thrilling ride that is best left to experts unless you enjoy plucking urchin spikes out of your body – or worse.

What's more, it hardly ever goes flat here. Although winter is bigger and more consistent (expect waves almost every day and rarely if ever below head high), even the height of summer will invariably see you score some decent action if you're in town for a few days.

Just to make things a little more difficult, you should note that most peaks will be 'crowded' even with just a handful of surfers in the water, as the take-off zones are small. And the water is surprisingly chilly considering Iquique's location, although that is tempered somewhat by a climate that is pleasantly warm and sunny year round.

For lesser mortals the area doesn't really offer much of a welcome in terms of waves – even the surf on the city's Cavancha Beach is heavy and hollow and prone to closing out – but serious surfers looking to visit somewhere very different in every sense of the word could do a lot worse than pay a call. Just remember to bring a spare board and a ding repair kit.

Difficulty
Expert

Hazards
Big, heavy waves;
shallow; rocks; sea
urchins; remote

Season
Year round

Water temperature
17–22°C (62–72°F)

Wetsuit
3/2 steamer or shortie;
boardshorts feasible in
summer; boots useful
for rock hopping

Access
Expensive flights; access
on island very variable,
with good road access to
some breaks but others
may require a hike;
getting in and out of the
surf tricky at most breaks

Other local breaks
None

While you're there
Obviously check out the
stone heads; visit Ranu
Raraku, for instance,
where the heads are
carved from the hillside

EASTER ISLAND
Get ahead of the pack on Rapa Nui

Few places on Earth provide such an esoteric surfing destination as Easter Island or, to use its local and far more exotic name, Rapa Nui. This small dot of sharp volcanic rock in the middle of the Pacific lies almost as exposed to swell as the Hawai'ian islands thousands of miles to the north, and has almost as rich a surfing history; and, of course, it also has its remarkable stone heads, or 'moia'.

These are not unlike the surf: huge and solid and emanating a dispassionate sense of power. As with the swells that pound the island, there's always the feeling that they're watching you, ready to pounce when you're least ready.

Rapa Nui swells can increase in size frighteningly quickly and, while few spots here are ever really relaxing to surf, it's not unusual for a relatively relaxed, slightly overhead session to develop into an epic. The waves build remorselessly, insensitive to riders' limits and equally uncaring of the consequences of a pounding wipeout onto the sharp, shallow rocks and reefs over which virtually all the island's waves break.

So, the world's most remote inhabited island is clearly not a place to be taken lightly. But whilst Rapa Nui's waves are likely to prove a challenge, you are at least unlikely to find yourself fighting for a place in the lineup. The combination of big, serious waves, a small population and expensive flights have conspired to ensure that while 'modern' surfing has been enjoyed on Rapa Nui since the '80s, it's still a minority sport.

The island's earlier inhabitants were surfing here on basic wooden craft hundreds of years ago, following the example set by sea turtles they saw riding in the waves. The antecedents of today's surfers were often forced to use materials such as old wooden doors, expensive fibreglass boards being in short supply, and this clearly limited the seriousness of the waves they could take on. Fortunately, they can now access proper boards.

Rapa Nui's only settlement of Hanga Roa on the west coast is the focal point for both local and visiting surfers, and it has a couple of relatively mellow breaks that are ridden by sensible visitors getting their first feel for the place and by young islanders doing the same.

After this there's a virtually endless supply of options, especially on the south coast, but here the waves are likely to be big and powerful, often breaking on shallow rock shelves or in front of urchin covered rocks, so not only do you need a big wave gun, you also need the skills to use it properly.

Try heading to a break called Viringa o Tuki for your first taster. It has a more forgiving take off and is not as fast as the other breaks in the area, making for a good introduction. After this, ask the invariably friendly locals for advice; localism has yet to rear its head on Rapa Nui and hopefully may never do so.

Chile

Argentina   Uruguay

Mar del Plata

Atlantic
Ocean

Difficulty
Beginner – expert

Hazards
Crowds and localism;
some theft

Season
Year round but autumn/
winter best

Water temperature
10–20°C (50–68°F)

Wetsuit
5/3mm steamer, boots
and gloves in winter;
summer steamer or
shortie in summer

Access
Good road access to most
popular spots; and you
can take shorter boards
on public buses

Other local breaks
South of Necochea, you'll
find some good big wave
spots such as Los Angeles
and Cueva del Tigre

While you're there
Pay a visit to Buenos
Aires; the faded glory
of its boulevards and
mansions sits well with
the smouldering sexiness
of its nightclubs and
tango shows

MAR DEL PLATA, ARGENTINA

Catch a few along the coastline of South America's sleeping giant

For a country that boasts a vast stretch of Atlantic coastline that faces directly into the line of fire of Roaring Forties swells that provide surf year round, Argentina has always had a surprisingly low profile on the international surfing scene. That situation is only changing slowly, which may be no bad thing in these days of ever crowded waves.

The epicentre of Argentinian surfing is Mar del Plata, one of the country's foremost beach resorts, with a population of 600,000, most of whom appear to surf on summer days when the sun shines and the swell is small.

Located on a south–south-east facing bulge of coastline some 250 miles south of the capital of Buenos Aires, the coastline either side of the city is in the direct firing line of southern hemisphere swells and the large and surf frenzied population likes to make the most of them.

So, while this means the breaks can get very busy, on the plus side it also means that surfing the Mar del Plata region acts as a great and easily accessible introduction to South America's second largest country. If you want to escape the crowds, all you need do is head south.

The further you go the more solitude you'll find, until eventually you roll into Patagonia and Tierra del Fuego where vast expanses of empty and remote cold water surf spots await.

But back to the warmer waters of Mar del Plata...

The 100-mile stretch of coastline between Santa Clara del Mar just north of Mar del Plata and the city of Necochea to the south offers a huge selection of breaks, varying from the zoo-like La Popular in downtown Mar del Plata, which lives up to its name, to classy beach breaks such as Mariano just south of the city, or outstanding point breaks such as the long, rocky right at the aptly named Paradise some 15 miles south.

Many of the more accessible breaks have suffered in recent years, due to the installation of groynes along some stretches of beachfront, especially north of the city, but when there's a good swell running in conjunction with offshore winds from the north, you should have no trouble finding a wave to suit. This is particularly so if you can drag yourself out of bed at the crack of dawn; because Mar del Plata is a party town, those who can resist the temptation to hit the clubs can be paddling out into quiet lineups and offshore conditions when their fellow surfers are staggering homewards and won't be fit for anything until at least late morning.

Like so many other places, the prime surf season is winter, from March to November. Although you must endure relatively cold water temperatures at this time of year, the waves are considerably quieter than in summer as well, being more consistent and bigger.

Paraguay

Argentina

Uruguay

Atlantic
Ocean

Difficulty
Beginner – expert

Hazards
Crowds and localism at
some breaks

Season
Year round but autumn/
winter best

Water temperature
12–22°C (53–72°F)

Wetsuit
5/3mm steamer, boots
and gloves in winter;
summer steamer or
shortie in summer

Access
Good road access to most
popular spots

Other local breaks
Head north into Brazil and
you'll find no shortage
of waves

While you're there
Make like a gaucho and
visit one of the country's
tourist estancias

URUGUAY

Small is beautiful in
South America's tiniest nation

Uruguay is South America's smallest country and, with only 140 miles of Atlantic
Ocean shoreline (as opposed to an additional 280 miles that fronts the estuary of the
River Plate and receives little if any surf), it is the one country on the continent that you
can check out easily in a few days.

Tucked away as it is between the giants of Brazil and Argentina, Uruguay has remained
something of a surfing backwater, which for many surf travellers can only be a good
thing. This doesn't mean that you'll have all the waves to yourself, of course, but it does
make for a somewhat less hyper surf scene than, for instance, Mar del Plata in nearby
Argentina (see p138).

You'll find a healthy selection of waves all the way, from the country's main beach
resort of Punta del Este at the mouth of the River Plate, to Barra del Chuy on the
Brazilian border, with the swells mainly throwing themselves ashore on sandy beaches
such as Chiberta in Punta del Este and La Aguada in the town of La Paloma, which is
especially popular with beginners.

That said, there are a few decent reefs and points to be found, La Derecha to the north-east of La Paloma being one of the better reef breaks and La Barra near Punta del Este providing two of the best point breaks in the country.

Despite facing south-east, Uruguay isn't noted for attracting the big swells birthed by the Roaring Forties, and waves of between two and four feet are common although bigger waves are quite frequent in winter.

This combination of smaller swells, relatively undemanding waves, easily accessed coastline (just an hour or so from the international airport at Montevideo) and a temperate climate that rarely if ever sees temperatures fall below freezing makes for a very user-friendly surf experience in what is quite an exotic location even if only for its lack of exposure.

Seeing and being seen is a large part of the Uruguayan beach scene, with hundreds of thousands of visitors arriving each summer from Brazil and Argentina to boost the local crowds from Montevideo. A large proportion of that number appear to be toting surfboards and all the attendant gear, but be not alarmed; for many of them, it's as much about looking the part in front of the girls in bikinis as tearing the surf apart, and competition for waves will not be as fierce as you would expect once out in the water.

Which all goes to prove that even in a continent of huge countries, small can still be beautiful − and well worth a visit.

Brazil

Bolivia

Paraguay

Santa Catarina

Uruguay

Difficulty
Beginner – expert

Hazards
Some crowded breaks;
urchins at rocky breaks;
surfing may be banned
on some beaches during
May–June fishing season;
some minor theft

Season
March – October

Water temperature
17–24°C (63–75°F)

Wetsuit
3/2 steamer in winter;
shortie or boardshorts
and rash vest in summer

Access
Good road access to the
most popular breaks;
others may require four-
wheel drive or hike

Other local breaks
Head south to Uruguay
(see p140) for smaller but
quieter waves

While you're there
If you're on a tight budget
head into Florianopolis,
where the traditional
churrasqueria rodizio
steak houses offer an
all-you-can eat meat
experience that will fill
you up after the longest
of surf sessions

SANTA CATARINA ISLAND, BRAZIL

Something for everyone in Brazil's surf capital

The 20-mile long, jaggedy shaped island of Santa Catarina lies off the coast of southern Brazil, connected by bridge to the city of Florianopolis and with the best and most consistent surf in the country. Not only this, but it's open to a big swell window of 225°, which means that when there's a good swell it'll almost certainly be offshore somewhere.

Add in a generally more cosmopolitan environment that's easier for travellers to adapt to than that of many more rural areas of Brazil, along with a pretty amenable sub-tropical climate, and all sounds well with the surfing world in Santa Caterina.

There's just one minor irritant in that the water is not as warm as you might expect in a country known for its hot and sunny climate, and you'll probably find a full suit necessary if surfing here in winter. But that's a small price to pay for the consistency and quality of waves at this time of year.

If you surf in winter you'll also find far fewer surfers in the water. Summer sees visitors from all over Brazil and further afield flocking to the coast, many of them toting boards, and you can expect popular sandy beaches such as Joaquina to be jammed.

This is the surf capital of southern Brazil so you wouldn't expect it to be anything less than hectic at this time of year but, since it can hold real quality swells up to well overhead in size, you'll find that waves are to be had on bigger days when less experienced surfers are struggling with the conditions.

And even in summer you can avoid the worst of the hordes. Head north to the nine-mile stretch of sands that makes up Moçambique Beach and you'll find classic empty peaks with walls racing left and right.

Things get noticeably quieter as you head towards the southern end of Santa Catarina, which is much more rural and has a feel of old Portugal about it. Here you'll hit upon a range of exposed beach and point breaks that will always be quieter than their neighbours to the north since you have to hike to them.

Santa Catarina's small size may leave you feeling that you need to expand your horizons after a few days here, and you could do far worse than make the short trip over to the mainland and head south towards the town of Imbituba, where you'll find one of the best rivermouth breaks in the country at Guarda do Embau as well as an excellent big wave spot in the form of Praia da Vila, on a headland to the south of the town.

So, one island, one short stretch of mainland coast and something for everyone – not a bad mix, hey?

China

Sea of Japan
(East Sea)

Tokyo

Japan

Kyushu

Difficulty
Beginner – expert

Hazards
More popular breaks can
be crowded; urchins on
rocky reefs

Season
Late summer

Water temperature
15–25°C (59–77°F)

Wetsuit
4/3mm steamer in winter;
shortie or boardshorts in
summer; boots useful on
rocky reefs

Access
Good road access to more
popular spots but many
stretches of coastline
are virtually inaccessible
without a boat

Other local breaks
If you fancy a little
exploration, head to the
island of Tenegashima
off the southern coast for
much quieter waves

While you're there
There are six national
parks on the island
so take some hiking
boots for when the surf
goes flat

KYUSHU, JAPAN

Warm waves, sub-tropical weather and plenty of breaks on Kyushu Island

The most southerly of Japan's four main islands has a healthy stash of breaks, and while the easterly Pacific coast is by far the most wave favoured coastline, there is also surf to be found on the west coast in the East China Sea and the north coast in the Sea of Japan.

For any western surfer, the chance to surf these two exotic sounding seas alone is perhaps reason enough to visit, although you'll inevitably end up spending most of your time on the east coast since its wide swell window and deep offshore waters are ideal for kicking up quality waves year round.

As with the rest of Japan, it's late summer that brings the biggest and most consistent surf, with typhoon season in full swing. At this time of year you may get typhoon swells on both the west and east coasts, along with water temperatures as high as 25°C (77°F), and while it's unlikely you'll score empty waves, Kyushu is considerably less crowded than the islands to the north.

What's more, the better breaks, such as the long left hand reef point at Lena midway down the west coast or the challenging Curren's Point (named after former world champ Tom Curren) to the south of Miyazaki, are not favoured by the majority of local surfers who for reasons best known to themselves tend to prefer to hang around in groups on the island's beach breaks.

You may find that things are a tad quieter on the shores of the East China Sea since the surf here is less consistent, but summer typhoons crossing offshore towards China and Korea can send some very acceptable pulses of swell rolling ashore, especially around the Nagasaki Peninsula.

The drive here from the Pacific coast is worth the journey even if the surf isn't as good as you were hoping for, since it takes in much of the island's spectacular topography of wild coastline and spectacular volcanic uplands, as well as travelling past ancient Buddhist shrines and through traditional towns and villages (Kyushu is often referred to as the cradle of Japanese culture).

If you're on the island in winter when the east coast is taking a battering from Pacific storms and may even be unsurfable, consider a trip to the north coast, which can have some first rate beach and reef breaks thanks to strong northerly swells running down the Sea of Japan, and the island's sub-tropical climate means there's no real discomfort in paddling out in a decent wetsuit.

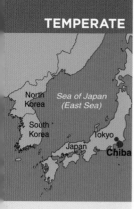

Difficulty
Beginner – expert

Hazards
Very crowded; some
water pollution possible

Season
Late summer – autumn

Water temperature
13–22°C (55–72°F)

Wetsuit
Winter steamer and boots
to shortie or boardshorts

Access
Good road access to most
main breaks although
traffic can be heavy

Other local breaks
Head north of Chōshi for
less crowded waves

While you're there
Spend some time in
Tokyo, it may well blow
your mind; or head south
to the perfect cone of
Japan's most sacred
mountain, Mount Fuji

CHIBA PENINSULA, JAPAN

Tokyo's surf beaches can be crowded and crazy, but still worth a visit

OK, first the bad news: the Chiba Peninsula is located just to the east of Tokyo, which has a population of almost 13 million. And for a good proportion of that population, the peninsula's breaks are well under an hour's drive away. So you'll have surmised that the waves can get pretty busy hereabouts.

Now for the good news: catch a late summer swell when the water is a balmy 20°C (68°F) plus, the air is even warmer and the peninsula's breaks can have some size and power, and the numbers in the water will lessen remarkably, so there's a reasonable chance of scoring a few quality rides.

The crowds here can be phenomenal at summer weekends, though the Japanese are nothing if not sociable when it comes to surfing and seem to love sitting nose to tail (literally) in the lineup. So the best time to hit the surf is midweek, when most of the weekend warriors are ensconced behind their desks in Tokyo.

You'll probably want to ensure you visit in summer, since the seasonal variations in climate and water temperature are pretty marked. While late August can see you paddling out comfortably in a shortie or even boardshorts, take on the same waves four months later and you'll need a thick layer of neoprene and booties.

Prime spots include the relatively powerful and reasonably uncrowded beach breaks at Chōshi in the north of the peninsula; Big Ben, where swells are funnelled into the beach by a deep water channel; and the quality river-mouth break of Wada.

The best surf comes courtesy of the region's summer typhoons, which roughly speaking hit the area between June and late October. Unfortunately, these are not predictable enough to be able to guarantee you waves unless you're in the area for weeks rather than days, but catch a good typhoon swell and you can expect to score well overhead waves at many beaches.

While some would understandably consider the close proximity of Tokyo to be a negative aspect of surfing in this region, it really ought to be seen as one of the benefits. After all, there are few other surf zones in the world that are so close to such a fascinating, eclectic and bizarre city, and few surfers would visit the area intending only to ride waves as there are better regions of the Land of the Rising Sun in which to do that, such as Kyushu (see p144).

As a foreigner you'll have few problems making new friends as even in these days of relatively cheap and easy overseas travel not that many western surfers visit Japan; and your new found friends will certainly be intent on ensuring you get the best out of both the waves and the nearby city.

China

North Korea

Sea of Japan (East Sea)

South Korea

Cheju-Do

Difficulty
Beginner – expert

Hazards
Some shallow lava rock reefs; popular breaks can be crowded in summer

Season
August – November

Water temperature
12–24°C (53–75°F)

Wetsuit
Boardshorts and rash vest in summer, 3/2 or 4/3 steamer rest of year; boots useful in winter and on reefs

Access
Popular breaks generally easy to access by road

Other local breaks
The Japanese island of Fukuoka to the east gets decent autumn and winter surf and is warmer than Cheju-Do

While you're there
Check out the amazing lava caves (basically a lava tube), some of which are several miles long; Cheju-Do's bizarre volcanic landscape is one reason it's been declared a World Heritage Site

JUNGMUN BEACH, CHEJU-DO, SOUTH KOREA

Get tubed in more ways than one in South Korea

The Yellow Sea isn't the most appealing name for the body of water that bestows waves upon the golden sands of Jungmun Beach, but fortunately the sea isn't actually yellow and neither are the waves.

Indeed, the translucent green walls of water that funnel into the bay here are both warm and inviting, and for local surfers and scores of visiting Japanese wave riders this is almost the late summer equivalent of south-west France for their European counterparts.

At this time of year the waters allow boardshort surfing, the swells are at their cleanest, biggest and most consistent and the weather is hot. Unfortunately, it can also be pretty humid if not downright wet, although that eases off as you move into autumn, and while the swells that hit the island of Cheju-Do on which Jungmun is to be found are rarely that big or long lived, a visit of a couple of weeks would see you pretty sure of scoring some fun waves.

But there's more to Cheju-Do than just a selection of hollow beach breaks at Jungmun Beach. While this is the centre of surfing on the island, with a surf club and even regular comps, those searching for quieter and more challenging waves would do well to use Jungmun as an introduction to the area before heading off on a surfari along the south coast.

Within a strip of just a few miles you'll find a variety of breaks, varying from the hard to reach (and therefore crowd free) left hander of Squid Point at the south-west tip of the island to the fast lefts and rights of Shilla Point just west of Jungmun.

There's also a series of easy beach breaks on the north shore although these tend to be rather mushy and don't often work outside winter, when water temperatures dip to chilly levels and it'll be mainly locals who are in the water.

The time to visit, if you can, is when a summer typhoon swell is bearing down on the island (as opposed to the typhoon itself) since this will provide plenty of power and size at the known spots and may also stir a few 'unknown' spots into life, making a bit of exploration well worth while; for while there's a growing and enthusiastic surf population on the island most locals are happy to stick to the regular breaks and aren't over interested in exploration.

But don't expect consistent swell on Cheju-Do. Look instead to enjoy frequent but short lived swells of a day or two in duration and take full advantage of the days off to discover something of the eclectic culture and landscape of this southern outpost of the Korean Peninsula.

Alaska

Anchorage

North Pacific Ocean

Canada

USA

Difficulty
Expert

Hazards
Cold; remote; bears;
orcas; powerful swells;
rocks; currents

Season
Year round in theory,
although winter is too
harsh for most

Water temperature
Minus 1–16°C (30–60°F)

Wetsuit
Steamer, boots,
gloves and hood
for most of the year

Access
Difficult

Other local breaks
They're out there
to be discovered
by the hundred

While you're there
Enjoy the wilderness:
hiking, fishing, whale
watching – it's all there
in Alaska

ALASKA

Is this still the 'Last Frontier'?

Alaska is often called the 'Last Frontier' and while the truly wild and often pristine environment that is synonymous with the state can surely justify this, perhaps the region is no longer surfing's last frontier. After all, there's at least one surf shop here now.

The USA's largest state is bigger than all but 18 countries on Earth, which means it can still be a very long journey to buy a block of surf wax. Even so, surfing is now established as a small part of Alaska's outdoor culture.

There are obvious reasons for this, provided you have a good wetsuit. The massive coastline (more than the rest of the USA put together) of beaches, bays, coves and promontories facing every which way is washed by surf year round; the waters are crystal clear and way 'warmer' than you might expect this far north; and if you want solitude, it's easier to find than falling off your board. In fact, outside of a handful of established surf spots, you're more likely to have to share your waves with bears, seals or orcas than humans.

The focal points of Alaskan surfing are Hinchinbrook and Montague Islands to the west of the town of Cordova, and the small settlement of Yakutat, where the Icy Waves Surf Shop exhorts visiting surfers to contact the score or so of locals who will be happy to show them where the best surf is to be found because '...it can get lonely out there.' There is also a small surf community on the even more remote Kodiak Island on the west side of the Gulf of Alaska.

There are some readily accessed surf spots in the Yakutat area, such as Ocean Cape and Point Carrew, which can see a handful of surfers out on most decent days, and the islands of the Alexander Archipelago to the south are ideally placed to pick up swells rolling in from south and west; but a local guide is invaluable for finding the best waves in such areas, as are a rugged four-wheel drive vehicle, some sort of boat or best of all a float plane, all of which can be procured if you have the money.

Once you get out to these areas you need to be totally self-sufficient. But for anyone who loves wild northern landscapes and an almost infinite selection of empty line ups, is willing to make a big effort and lay down a lot of cash, surfing in Alaska is a unique experience that you'll remember for the rest of your life.

Canada

Vancouver

Tofino

North
Pacific
Ocean

USA

TOFINO, VANCOUVER ISLAND, BRITISH COLUMBIA

Watch out for the wildlife

Difficulty
Beginner – expert

Hazards
Cold in winter; some
breaks very remote;
rips and currents; bears
and orcas

Season
Year round

Water temperature
9–16°C (48–60°F)

Wetsuit
Full steamer, boots and
gloves in winter; 3/2
steamer may be possible
in summer

Access
Varies from excellent
to needing a boat or
floatplane for backcountry
breaks north of Tofino

Other local breaks
Endless discoveries to be
made to the north

While you're there
There are some good
hiking trails through the
forests; in winter, Mount
Washington has some
of the highest snowfall
in Canada and is a good
skiing/boarding option

It's isn't often that you're not at the top of the food chain both in and out of the water, but that's very much the case on Vancouver Island. Here, spectacular forests tumble down to the sea from high mountains and are home to bears, wolves and mountain lions, while out at sea killer whales and sea lions are just two species you'll be sharing the water with.

But no surfers are known to have been eaten or otherwise abused to date – which is maybe just as well since the waves of Vancouver Island can be challenging enough.

The enthusiastic surfing population of Tofino and Ucluelet, its blue collar neighbour to the south, rarely gets excited unless a swell with a period in excess of 18 seconds starts rolling ashore, which means there's plenty of power to the waves. They may have travelled all the way from the southern hemisphere before thumping ashore at spots such as Long Beach or Cox Bay, and that's given them plenty of time to get their act together and line up like the ranks of an invading army before marching ashore.

The area around Tofino is now Canada's answer to Newquay, Huntington and Manly. Admittedly it is far less busy than any of these but it is essentially Surf Central, Canada, and as such is full to overflowing with surf shops, surf bars, surfers and all things wave oriented.

But it has a cool and enthusiastic vibe, from beginners in from Vancouver for their first shot at wave riding to hardcore locals such as the unassuming Pete Devries, winner of the area's first pro surf contest (much to the unbridled delight of Tofino's resident surf community) and the Bruhwiler brothers, keen surf explorers who regularly travel north by boat to search out waves that First Nation people may have known about for centuries but are only now being surfed.

Indeed, this territory to the north, roadless and untamed, has changed little since Captain George Vancouver sailed these shores over 200 years ago, and there's a palpable sense of First Nation culture and the power of nature as you travel along these shorelines and through the forests above.

You can also feel the raw power of nature out in the waves. Even on a head high day, the Pacific Ocean hereabouts can pack a punch. If you paddle out in winter when a gentle breeze drifts snowflakes out to sea, the sea is milk white, the water is grey and the beach is black, the only relief from the monochrome environment in which you're immersed comes from the verdant green of the forests, which are absolutely integral to everything about this glorious corner of the globe.

But take off on one of these muscled swells as it booms ashore and your world bursts into life and colour as, for a few seconds at least, you get as close to nature as the Nuu-chah-nulth people who inhabited these shores long before surfers 'discovered' them.

Canada

Seattle

Washington

Difficulty
Beginner (at less
exposed, less remote
spots) – expert

Hazards
Cold water and risk
of hypothermia; wild
climate; currents;
remote breaks; sharks

Season
Year round

Water temperature
6–17°C (42–62°F)

Wetsuit
Full winter steamer,
boots, gloves and hood
in winter; 4/3 or 3/2
steamer in summer

Access
Fly into Seattle, rent a car
and head for the coast

Other local breaks
Good waves in Oregon
to the south and on
Vancouver Island in
British Columbia

While you're there
The windy coastline
makes kite flying popular;
check out the World
Kite Museum at Long
Beach and the annual
international kite festival
held in the third week
of August

WASHINGTON STATE, USA

Wild, wet and windy but plenty of waves in Washington State

If anything, the Washington coastline is even wilder than that of Oregon to the south; in fact, surfers here are lucky to have the relatively sheltered northern coast of the Straits of Juan de Fuca, which will often have good waves when the more exposed Pacific coast to the south is being battered by huge, unsurfable storm swells that regularly exceed 20–30 ft.

There are few settlements of any real size on this coastline, which means the pristine – albeit very wet – landscape has retained much of its beauty. Surfing here, you're very much aware of being surrounded by raw, elemental nature.

This is particularly so in the north of the state where the lush, green temperate rain forests of the Olympic National Park rise above a rocky coastline to which access is very limited. Other than the residents of the Native American reservations in the area, it's fair to say there are probably more bear, moose and elk living here than humans. Out at sea the wildlife is equally full on, with sharks, cetaceans and sea lions making up a good chunk of the larger marine life.

The south of the state is more accessible and consists of magnificent wide beaches littered with huge drifts of lumber interspersed with the deep blue bays of Grays Harbour and Willapa Bay.

But the Pacific is, in general, a non-winter surf zone simply because winter swells are often just too big and menacing to be realistically surfable. Look to head here in late August or September for prime conditions, when a small summer swell, warm weather and gentle offshore breeze may combine to produce memorable beach break sessions at popular spots such as Westport between Grays Harbour and Willapa Bay, or off 28-mile Long Beach just north of the Columbia River estuary.

When things start to get wild, it's time to head north to the Straits of Juan De Fuca, where north-west swells roll ashore onto a variety of beach, reef and point breaks below the Canadian border and offer the chance to explore for lesser known spots.

The swells need to be big to get into the relatively sheltered spots here, which means it's more consistent in winter, but it's possible to get a decent north-west groundswell at any time of year so don't regard these spectacular waters as out of bounds in the warmer months.

Wherever you choose to surf in this part of the world, don't forget to bring good foul-weather gear with you, particularly hiking boots and a rain jacket. Howling gales and driving rain may well accompany you both in and out of the surf, which ensures that, while both relatively surf rich and incredibly wild and beautiful, Washington State will always be a surf destination for more adventurous wave riders.

Difficulty
Intermediate – expert

Hazards
Cold water and risk
of hypothermia; wild
climate; currents; remote
breaks; sharks

Season
Year round

Water temperature
8–11°C (46–52°F)

Wetsuit
Full winter steamer,
boots, gloves and hood
in winter; gloves and
hood may not be
required in summer

Access
Fly into Eugene to the
east of Florence, rent a car
and head for the coast

Other local breaks
Nelscott Reef to the north
of the state is a classic
big wave venue – expert
only, though

While you're there
Try sandboarding on
the largest expanse of
coastal sand dunes in
North America to the
south of Florence

SOUTHERN OREGON, USA

Grab a thick wetsuit and a warm lumberjack shirt to fit in with the locals

The rugged coast of Southern Oregon is one of the most remote and wild places
in the USA; the thick pines of the Siskiyou National Forest tumble down to driftwood
strewn coves and beaches, summer wildflowers add a splash of bright colour to the ever
present green of woods, fields and waves, and crystal clear rivers burst forth from the hills
to provide river-mouth breaks where the slight inconvenience of the occasional shark
hasn't been enough to deter hardcore locals from riding the waves year round.

The verdant landscape is watered by heavy rains, often accompanied by wild winds,
especially in winter, so you need to be prepared in terms of both gear and attitude before
surfing here. The payoff is that you get to enjoy quiet, powerful breaks where the locals
are generally pretty mellow as long as you are. And they have their secret spots too, of
course, which it's highly unlikely you'll get to hear about.

Heading north from the Oregon/California state line to the attractive historic town of
Florence, which sits pretty much on the 44° latitude line, you'll discover around 200 miles
of inspirational coastline offering a range of beach, reef and point breaks, with beach
breaks in the ascendancy.

Depending on the size of the swell and the direction of the wind – predominantly
south in winter, north-west in summer – there can be waves to suit everyone from
beginner to expert, although on bigger swells it helps to be a powerful paddler and duck
diver to negotiate the lines of white water on the beach breaks.

This, and the fact that the water never even gets close to warm, can make surfing in
Oregon a stern test of fitness and commitment, all sound reasons for the kind of crowds
associated with California to the south not being a major issue here.

Your surfing location will depend on the season. In winter, both wind and swell come
predominantly from the west, so ideally you need to search out breaks facing north-
west, such as Bastendorf Beach at Coos Bay. In summer, the predominant swell direction
becomes north-west, as do the winds, so look for waves at spots such as Brookings near
the state border or Battle Rock near Port Orford, which is a good option on big swells.

Whenever you visit, a surf trip to Southern Oregon is a real adventure. The easy life of
chilling out on the beach after a session that is part and parcel of more traditional surf
trips isn't the way it's done here. You'll want to keep moving to keep warm on all but the
sunniest of summer days, but that's no bad thing since it gives you every excuse to keep
exploring this wild and beautiful coastline.

And who knows, you may just find a Southern Oregon peak of your own.

Difficulty
Beginner – expert

Hazards
Cold water; powerful
waves on bigger swells;
shallow water on some
breaks; sharks; crowds

Season
Year round

Water temperature
12–16°C (53–61°F)

Wetsuit
3/2 or 4/3 steamer, boots

Access
Good road access
to most breaks

Other local breaks
Huge array of beach
breaks from Santa Cruz
for 12 miles all the way
to Moss Landing

While you're there
Visit the weird and
wacky Mystery Spot in
the redwood forests
just outside town, a
classic mad California
tourist attraction that
will bemuse you with
genuinely puzzling
variations of gravity,
perspective and height

SANTA CRUZ, NORTHERN CALIFORNIA

All hail Santa Cruz – it's where the surfer's wetsuit was created!

Santa Cruz is steeped in surf history and culture, from the surf museum above the break at Steamer Lane to the famous O'Neill Surf Shop, whose founder Jack O'Neill pioneered the modern wetsuit, so we all have much to thank him for.

But of course, none of that would be here without the waves, and the coastline hereabouts is blessed with an overabundance of them, not to mention the monster Mavericks just up the coast for committed big wave chargers, ideally equipped with a jet ski and tow-in partner.

Probably the most famous of the town's waves is Steamer Lane, which is actually a series of quality right hand point/reef breaks (with occasional long lefts) that break further out to sea as the swell gets bigger. Although it's a fairly user friendly wave, it's always busy with some excellent local surfers dominating the pack so you'll be hard pushed to get all

the waves you want. But paddle out anyway – even if you only catch one wave, at least
you can say you've surfed at one of California's most iconic surf spots.

And there are stacks of alternatives if Steamer Lane is too busy or too big for you.
Depending on swell and wind conditions, places like Cowells, inside 'The Lane', are good
for less confident surfers, and as you head south past the harbour and the main beach
frontage of the town there's a whole array of beach, point and reef breaks to suit all levels
of ability and riding styles; you'll see the full gamut of wave riding vehicles in use around
Santa Cruz, from longboards to body boards, shortboards to surf skis.

The Santa Cruz surf experience is about more than simply riding waves, though. Once
you've had your fill of action in the water, hit the surf museum. However little regard you
may have for 'culture' you'd have to be a real philistine not to be fascinated by the century
of local surf history on display here.

And, of course, there's the town itself, which is one of those great places where a dude
with wet hair, salt-red eyes and a board under his or her arm fits in just perfectly.

All of which makes Santa Cruz sound like a little bit of cold water surf perfection (if you
exclude the crowds). And in many cases it is, but there's one fly in the ointment – sharks.
Yes, the chances of ending up on the wrong end of a great white are slim, but this area is
a breeding ground for these guys so you need to bear that in mind.

But hey, forget the negative. If as a surfer you can't enjoy a trip to Santa Cruz it's
probably time to hang up your board and start playing darts...

Difficulty
Beginner – expert

Hazards
Cold water outside summer and risk of hypothermia; many remote breaks.

Season
March – December (prime season mid-August to mid-November)

Water temperature
0–23°C (32–73°F)

Wetsuit
Full winter steamer, boots, gloves and hood in winter; boardshorts in summer

Access
For the Upper Peninsula, fly into Grand Rapids or Traverse City and rent a car; access to breaks varies from paved roads to dirt tracks and walks through forest

Other local breaks
All five of the Great Lakes get surf

While you're there
In winter, continue the weirdness with a ski or snowboard trip to Shanty Creek Resort, an hour north of Traverse City, with a massive 450 ft of vertical

THE GREAT LAKES, USA/CANADA

Salt-free surfing on the world's largest freshwater lakes

Unless you're from North America you probably can't even name all five Great Lakes (Superior, Huron, Michigan, Erie and Ontario) so it's unlikely you'll ever have thought about surfing these freshwater 'inland seas'.

But they do get surf on occasion and while it will never compare to a real ocean swell there's still something pretty cool about riding waves in what are surfing backwaters in every sense of the word.

Don't be fooled into thinking that as mere lakes the waves here will never be more than a languid ripple. Lake Superior is the world's largest freshwater lake and as such can create its own weather systems, which are occasionally ferocious. One storm in November 1975 saw hurricane force winds generating vessel-sinking waves in excess of 20 ft.

While all the lakes can get waves from time to time, probably the most consistent body of water is Lake Michigan, around the Upper Peninsula area in the north, which also has the advantage of being within easy reach of Lake Superior and Lake Huron.

Low pressure systems tracking across the lakes will generate swell that you can generally expect to be less powerful than an ocean swell of equivalent size. And don't forget that fresh water is around 20% less buoyant than salt water, which will affect your surfing, so consider riding a bigger board to make up for the lack of buoyancy.

Because of the geography of the peninsula, the winds that create any swell will be offshore somewhere, so there's a decent chance you'll find a sheltered beach or point where the waves can wrap around to produce something approaching a decent wall that, particularly on a longboard or mini-mal, can be ridden for some distance.

Wave periods tend to be short, rarely over nine or ten seconds, due to the limited fetch of all the lakes, so expect waves similar to summer wind swells off, say, Cornwall or Brittany. But at most spots you won't have to deal with the crowds that are common on the coast – in fact, you'll be greeted by incredibly enthusiastic locals, the most committed of whom will paddle out in winter conditions when the water is close to freezing and the air is well below. Madness!

But then, there's a somewhat surreal air about everything to do with Great Lakes surfing. Here you are, hundreds of miles from the coast, having driven through bucolic farmland or snowy forests to access the shoreline of a lake so big you may not be able to see the opposite shore. It leaves you trying to remember at times whether you're on the coast or not, although a quick taste of the water will soon put you right.

Catch it lucky, though, and you could find that the Great Lakes provide you with one of your more memorable surfing adventures, as much because it's all so off the wall as anything.

New York

Long Island

Philadelphia

North Atlantic Ocean

Difficulty
All standards

Hazards
Crowds; traffic; cold winters

Season
Year round

Water temperature
4–20°C (39–68°F)

Wetsuit
Steamer, boots, gloves and hood in winter; boardshorts possible in summer/autumn

Access
Easy, although traffic and parking can be a problem

Other local breaks
Check out Cape Cod to the north and Atlantic City to the south

While you're there
Simple – visit the Big Apple; if you're there in September, check out the New York Surf Film Festival

LONG ISLAND, NEW YORK STATE

Living for the city and the surf

For many surfers, the demands of work and having to live close to your workplace are a definite hindrance when it comes to logging wave time. Well, no such excuses if you live in the Big Apple – hop on the subway and within less than half an hour you can be whisked from the heart of one of the world's most exciting cities to the heart of a late summer hurricane swell.

New York City's tentacles stretch along the aptly named 188-mile Long Island for some distance, eventually fading away so that at the island's far north-eastern tip, the plush Hamptons and the points and coves of Montauk offer some of the most exclusive wave-washed real estate in the USA. Closer to the city, things are anything but exclusive, but waves know no social or geographical boundaries and just as readily roll ashore here within view of the famous New York skyline.

There are poignant images of 9/11 that capture surfers riding waves on Long Island as the Twin Towers burned in the distance. These waves probably saved more than one life,

since a number of the guys in the water had bunked off work in the World Trade Center to make the most of a quality late summer swell combined with warm, sunny conditions.

Long Island's coastline has a selection of beach and point breaks that in many ways mirror life in the nearby city, especially in summer; snarled up traffic, crowded beaches and frequently hot temperatures in and out of the surf don't make for the best of surf experiences. The coast reflects local surf culture, with plenty of surf shops, surf schools and even a surf museum, along with the kind of eclectic arts and music scene you'd expect this close to New York.

It's when everyone has gone back to work or school, however, that Long Island comes into its own. The south-east facing shoreline is ideally placed to mop up hurricane swells from the south and, while the long continental shelf does shave them of some of their power, it's not at all unusual in late summer and autumn to catch some quality waves in pleasantly mild waters, and without excessive crowds.

The city surfers here know to make the most of it because, come the winter, when snow on the beach is not uncommon and water temperatures are only a few degrees above freezing, you need real commitment to take on Long Island's surf. That said, you will find reasonably consistent surf if you can deal with the frigid temperatures.

Sure, Long Island is never going to be the purist's choice of surf spot, but if you want to combine city living with a surfing lifestyle it has lots to recommend it.

North Atlantic
Ocean

Difficulty
Beginner – expert

Hazards
Extremely cold in winter;
some breaks very remote;
rips and currents; moose

Season
Year round

Water temperature
1 - 16°C (33 - 60°F)

Wetsuit
Full winter steamer,
boots and gloves in
winter; 3/2 steamer
in summer

Access
Fly into Halifax and rent
a car; access to main
surf beaches generally
very good

Other local breaks
There's the potential to
make endless discoveries
along Nova Scotia's
south-east coast

While you're there
Enjoy a night out in
Halifax, which has one of
the coolest music scenes
in Canada and some
excellent bars

NOVA SCOTIA, CANADA
Beware of the snow

At the east end of Lawrencetown Beach, which is the hub of the Nova Scotia surf
scene, there's a road sign that advises motorists to "Beware of blowing snow" – not a
warning commonly seen above your regular surf beach.

But then, Nova Scotia is far from being a regular surf destination. It'll surprise no-one
to find that cold and snow go hand in hand with surf and surfboards here (hence the
road sign) and you do indeed need to be made of stern stuff – and/or have a serious
commitment to the sport – to surf year round in the province, but plenty do.

In summer, which is when most visitors are likely to find themselves here, it can be a
pure delight to ride Nova Scotia's waves. Long summer days, water temperatures in the
mid to high teens and sparkling blue waves feathering ashore onto golden sands mean
that you may have to keep reminding yourself you're in the land of Mounties, bears and
moose rather than on a Cornish beach.

The surfing population of Nova Scotia is focused on the cool city of Halifax and the
nearby beaches of Lawrencetown and Seaforth, where a few hundred mad keen surf

dudes (reduced in winter to a few score plain mad surf dudes) hang out at the beach or in the down home surf shops such as Happy Dudes, waiting for swells to arrive.

Ideal conditions tend to be associated with late summer hurricanes – not surprising, since air and water temperatures are at their highest then. With this will come crowds. Yes, the popular spots will be busy, but for anyone prepared to travel a little the chances to discover empty breaks are legion. Areas such as the spectacular Cape Breton Island offer endless kilometres of relatively unexplored coastline, while across the Cabot Strait is Newfoundland, which is as near as you'll get these days to virgin surf territory. A few hardy adventurers have ridden waves here, and if you want to surf alongside an iceberg with only a few seals and whales for company this is the place to do so.

Most of us are not that desperate to find surfing solitude, however, and will probably find the busier breaks near Halifax more than adequate. What's more, there's a great feel to the area. Although there have been surfers in Nova Scotia for decades it's only in recent years that the sport has taken off in any sense and there's still that sense of freshness and enthusiasm, and a warm welcome to visitors, that is all too sadly lacking in some more established surf spots.

Warm welcomes are all the more appreciated should you visit in the depths of winter, of course – in fact, anything warm will be appreciated then. And a snow shovel and snowshoes might also be worth tucking into your board bag.

Iceland
• Reykjavik

Atlantic Ocean

Difficulty
Good intermediate –
expert

Hazards
Cold air and water;
remote; currents;
shallow lava reefs

Season
April – September

Water temperature
3–15°C (37–59°F)

Wetsuit
Full steamer plus gloves,
boots and hood in colder
months; boots useful
year round, particularly
for walking over sharp
volcanic rocks

Access
Flights to Reykjavik; car
hire (ideally four-wheel
drive) essential

Other local breaks
n/a

While you're there
Explore the geysers,
hot springs, glaciers,
volcanoes and mountains
of this spectacular country

ICELAND

The waves are only half the thrill in Iceland's amazing landscapes

Like the Faroe Islands, Iceland lies in the path of virtually every storm and swell
that tracks across the North Atlantic, and its rugged coastline is something of a surf
magnet, albeit a cold, windswept and frequently inhospitable surf magnet.

Black volcanic sand beaches fringed by volcanic rock points and headlands create
an often monochrome shoreline, enlivened by the shimmer of gin clear waters above a
seabed that's a mix of smooth black sand and jagged solidified lava.

These somewhat challenging vistas are ameliorated by the warm welcome you'll
invariably receive from the score or so of local surfers, but don't necessarily expect them
to spill the beans on all the breaks.

It seems that these guys have learned the lessons of the past, when information on
surf spots once thought to be immune from overcrowding (such as those along Ireland's
west coast) was given freely and generously and, as a result, they now have dozens of
riders out on a good swell.

Iceland's locals clearly don't want their waves to suffer the same fate, although it's hard
to imagine the country's breaks ever seriously suffering from overcrowding. Factor in cold
water, hostile weather, a relatively short surf season (unless you're crazy enough to want to
surf in the few hours of daylight available in the frigid winter months – some locals do...),

inaccessibility and cost and everything mitigates against Iceland becoming the Hawai'i of the North Atlantic.

Visit in summer, however, when the water may be as 'warm' as 15°C (59°F), the air is milder and a clean, perfectly lined up groundswell is hitting the south coast after journeying thousands of miles from the south or south-west, and you may just think you've stumbled across a little surf nirvana.

Powerful, crystal clear overhead waves that barrel for hundreds of yards along points, reefs and beaches are not uncommon, but they can take some finding.

First port of call for visitors is the capital Reykjavik, easily one of the coolest cities in Europe and within easy reach of the eponymous Reykjanes Peninsula, the focal point of Icelandic surfing. You'll find a selection of readily accessible waves, for instance, at Grindavik, a small, attractive fishing port close to the famous Blue Lagoon thermal pools.

Also close by are breaks along the Sandgerdi coast and a decent point break at Thorlakshofn to the south-east. Depending on your predilection for exploring, you could well discover enough waves (and fellow surfers to share them with) between here and Reykjavik to keep you satisfied.

On the other hand, you could rent a four-wheel drive and explore. Iceland is a rather bizarre mix of incredibly civilized, cosmopolitan towns and villages interspersed with some of the wildest volcanic, glaciated and mountainous landscapes on Earth, plunging down to a coastline that is equally savage; any surfari here requires you to be pretty self-sufficient both in and out of the water.

But you don't have to be an explorer to be captivated by this mind-blowing country. Surf here and you'll still be one of very few to have done so – and unlike most other surf spots in this book, that's a situation that isn't likely to change much any time soon.

Lofoten
Islands

Norwegian
Sea

Finland

Sweden

Oslo

LOFOTEN ISLANDS, NORWAY

Arctic action in Norway's far north

Difficulty
Expert only

Hazards
Cold air and water; remote; currents (the infamous maelstrom tidal eddies are off the western coast); shallow cobble reefs

Season
April – September

Water temperature
3–10°C (37–50°F)

Wetsuit
Full steamer plus gloves, boots and hood

Access
Flights to Leknes, Svolvaer and Helle

Other local breaks
Who knows?

While you're there
There's some great mountaineering on the Lofoten Island's crags and peaks and even if you don't want actually to go rock climbing, it's worth bringing hiking boots

Situated at latitude 68-70°N and well within the Arctic Circle, the Lofoten Islands have the world's most northerly surf and are not the first place most people would associate with surfing.

However, individuals such as professional snowboarder Terje Haakonsen pioneered surfing here in the late 1990s and in more recent years the Rip Curl Search team and the amazing photos of professional surf photographer Yassine Wilal, who specializes in cold water destinations, have seen the Lofoten Islands getting exposure in surf magazines around the world.

Fortunately, the Gulf Stream still prevails this far north, preventing you and the water from literally freezing. In summer the sea may reach a balmy 10°C (50°F), which compares with winter in, say, south-west England – not warm but far from unbearable.

Thanks to its exposed location the archipelago receives lots of swell, although it doesn't usually get excessively big, and you can theoretically surf here for much of the year as long as you and your wetsuit can cope with water temperatures as low as 3°C (37°F). In the depths of winter surfing is out, though, since there's 24-hour darkness.

The prime season is in fact summer, not just because the weather is kinder then but also because this is when surfable groundswells tend to be more consistent. And, of course, you don't even have to take into account such issues as daylight at this time of year since the sun never slips below the horizon in midsummer.

Needless to say, crowds are not an issue, so you can head towards the few known surf spots such as Unstadt, Kvalnes and Eggum, safe in the knowledge that you can pick and choose any wave that comes through.

Surfing in the Lofoten Islands is about more than simply wave riding, however. Incredible coastlines of jade green waters, golden white sands and imposing cobble points pass inland into soaring, snow capped mountains rising up to almost 4,000 ft. Moose or otters may cross your tracks en route to the surf, sea eagles and puffins are common and, out at sea, orcas and other cetaceans are regularly spotted.

This being Norway, the wilderness is dotted with little oases of civilization like the attractive towns of Svolvaer and Leknes, where you'll find the luxuries of life such as restaurants and bars (albeit at frighteningly expensive Norwegian prices).

Indeed, the cost of a trip to Lofoten is another reason there will never be too many surfers riding the local waves, but you should look upon a visit here as being about travelling as much as surfing. This is a corner of the world that once visited is never forgotten, and any waves you may chance across are a bonus.

FAROE ISLANDS, NORTH ATLANTIC

Feel like a surf hero in landscapes right out of the Nordic sagas

Difficulty
Expert

Hazards
Remoteness; cold air and water; some breaks shallow and rocky; currents

Season
Spring – autumn

Water temperature
4 – 16°C (39 - 60°F)

Wetsuit
Winter steamer, plus gloves, boots and hood outside summer

Access
Car ferry and flights to the island capital Torshavn; car essential

Other local breaks
Explore and you'll find some

While you're there
The cool capital of Torshavn (pop. 19,000) has some great bars and restaurants, and has produced a number of excellent indie bands such as Orca and Boys in a Band

It takes just one glance at an atlas to see that the Faroe Islands are smack bang in the way of almost every low pressure system and swell that rolls across the North Atlantic, and are thus pounded by surf year round.

It takes a second glance at an atlas to see that this far north there will never be a day in the year when the waters here feel anything less than 'brisk'. But hey, modern wetsuits can deal just fine with such minor inconveniences, so bring your winter steamer with you and enjoy waves as they should be – empty of anyone other than you and your surf buddies.

This is only the half of the Faroes surf experience though. Paddle out, catch a few waves, then take time to sit back on your board and take in the epic landscape that surrounds you.

This is nature on a mind blowing scale, direct from the Nordic sagas. Gigantic sea cliffs and solitary sea stacks thrust up from the sea floor, ringed by seabirds tumbling and wheeling like rags thrown into the wind; misty waterfalls plummet hundreds of feet down black crags before being shredded apart by the winds; clouds spin around the snowy peaks of mountains that may never have had a human on their summit.

It's enough to distract you from your surfing. But like the scenery, the waves here deserve respect. They're cold, although not as cold as they might be, thanks to the Gulf Stream; they're powerful; and they're pretty incessant – it's a rare day that wind and waves don't bash into the Faroe Islands.

Only a handful of people have surfed the Faroes to date (there was one 'local' at the time of writing) and it's unlikely this remote enclave of Nordic civilization will ever suffer from crowded waves. Indeed, it's unlikely that all the breaks along the convoluted and often inaccessible 684 miles of coastline that make up the 18 islands of the Faroes will ever be discovered.

Don't be put off by what you see on the map, though. The Faroe islanders have put large wads of European Community money to good use, building a superb network of roads and sub-sea tunnels that allows you to get around with surprising ease by car, so a decent surfari is perfectly viable.

And it's not just the rare opportunity that the Faroes provide to find and even name an undiscovered break that makes the archipelago worth visiting. The locals – who almost all speak good English – are friendly enough anyway, but once they find out that you're in the islands to surf you'll get an extra warm welcome.

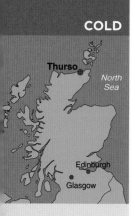

Difficulty
Expert

Hazards
Shallow water, rocks, cold air and water

Season
Year round

Water temperature
4 – 14°C (39 – 57°F)

Wetsuit
Winter steamer, plus gloves, boots and hood outside summer

Access
By car from Inverness

Other local breaks
The Shit Pipe and the beach just west of Thurso East are good options for less experienced surfers; Brimms Ness a few miles west has an even more challenging selection of reef breaks

While you're there
Take the ferry to the Orkneys – where you may also find good waves – to see the 5,000-year-old Neolithic houses at Skara Brae

THURSO EAST, NORTHERN SCOTLAND

Brave heart, not faint heart, will ensure you make the most of Scotland's best surf

Back in the early 1980s, the European Surfing Championships were held at Thurso East, in conditions that are pretty common here – clean, barrelling overhead waves, offshore winds and sunshine (well. . . , not that common in the case of the latter). And then Thurso quietly slipped back into something approaching obscurity for another 20 years.

The handful of locals and the occasional surf traveller venturing all the way to Scotland's chill grey northern coast were no doubt happy with this situation. After all, who wants to share one of the best rights in Europe if they don't have to? But, as with all good things, you can only keep them to yourself for so long.

Now Thurso is recognized as one of those places you must visit at some time in your surfing career – certainly if you're a British surfer, and plenty of more hardy dudes from warmer climates are also happy to don head-to-toe neoprene for the thrill of riding the area's steel blue waves.

Of a weekend, when there's a good swell, you'll have to compete to get the best waves with a cadre of hot locals who have it well sussed, along with surfers travelling up from all points south – in some cases as far south as Australia.

This situation has been exacerbated in recent years by exposure through O'Neill's Cold Water Classic event, which is held in the area every spring and has done a good job of showing the rest of the world that Scotland does indeed have world class waves.

And Thurso East is not a place for the faint hearted. It breaks in shallow water over flat, Caithness flagstone reefs draped in seaweed; it's fast and heavy; and you're weighed down by several pounds of wetsuit.

But if none of that phases you, you'll find a wave to remember, where getting covered up is the order of the day and the walls you're riding can easily get to three times overhead or bigger, as swells generated way up off the coast of Arctic Norway finally run aground.

As with all cold water surf spots, there's invariably a warm welcome in the water and in the local bars (try the Central Bar and Café on Traill Street). Places like Thurso generate a camaraderie amongst those who surf them because, even though it's busier in the water now than it's ever been, if you surf here you're still in a minority.

And if Thurso is too busy for you these days, well, simply head west along a coastline that becomes ever wilder and more spectacular to find a variety of breaks that are never likely to become too crowded.

Atlantic Ocean

Isle of Lewis

Isle of Harris

North Sea

Aberdeen

Edinburgh

Difficulty
Beginner – expert

Hazards
Remoteness; cold air
and water

Season
Spring – autumn

Water temperature
6 – 16°C (42 – 60°F)

Wetsuit
Winter steamer, plus
gloves, boots and hood
outside summer

Access
By car ferry from
Ullapool to Stornoway

Other local breaks
There are great waves and
similar surf conditions on
Tiree, one of the islands of
the Inner Hebrides

While you're there
Wildlife watching
boat trips to see seals,
cetaceans and seabirds
are available from Uig
on Lewis and Tarbert
on Harris

OUTER HEBRIDES, SCOTLAND

Spectacular Hebridean beaches promise great waves – but watch out for angry 'locals'

The wild and windswept islands of Lewis and Harris can be deceptive. Their glorious white sand beaches and limpid jade green waters look almost Caribbean and ought, from appearance, to be far warmer than they are.

That said, from a geographical point of view the seas here should actually be far colder than they are but, thanks to the Gulf Stream, the waves that roll ashore are bearable year round, and on a warm day in late summer you'd never guess you were at the same latitude as Labrador and Alaska.

Although these islands on the edge of Europe are not really the ideal place for novice surfers, there's enough variety of waves here for pretty much everyone. Beach breaks like Eòropaidh, when not too big, are ideal for learners to sample some of the most northerly surf they're ever likely to encounter, and there's even a surf school in the relatively cosmopolitan regional capital of Stornoway (www.hebrideansurf.co.uk), whose instructors

will hold your hand as you venture into the islands' crystal clear waters.

But the Outer Hebrides is really a destination for experienced surfers looking for empty waves and plenty of power. Barrelling beach breaks like Dalmore Bay and Bhaltos on Lewis, the hollow peaks rolling ashore on the huge golden crescent of Traigh Scarasta on Harris, or the point, reef and beach breaks along the west coast of the small archipelago of North Uist, Benbecula and South Uist may all pay huge dividends for those with the time to explore and a go-for-it attitude.

That said, you have to get your timing right. Although swells are pretty consistent throughout the year, so are the winds, which can come sweeping in from the North Atlantic like banshees and make a mess of the swell in double quick time. But on those days when the breeze swings offshore, the sun turns the waters a dappled turquoise and a clean, head high swell feathers onto the islands' deserted beaches, you really wouldn't want to be anywhere else.

Needless to say, facilities in this remote corner of Britain are pretty limited and you'll find that many stores and bars are closed on Sundays. There are of course very few locals, so if you do meet anyone when you're out in the water you'll more than likely get a warm welcome and some useful tips about other surf spots in the islands.

Not all the locals are friendly, though; ground nesting snowy white Arctic terns reside above many beaches and will dive bomb you to draw your attention away from their nests like a scene from Hitchcock's The Birds, which can be a tad unsettling as you stroll down to the surf. Maybe the few local surfers have put them up to it to ensure their waves never get too busy?

BUNDORAN, COUNTY SLIGO, IRELAND

Enjoy the waves and the 'craic' in Ireland's surf rich north-west

Difficulty
Beginner – expert

Hazards
Cold air and water (especially in winter); shallow and rocky on the reef breaks; powerful waves

Season
Year round but spring – autumn optimum

Water temperature
8–16°C (46–61°F)

Wetsuit
Full steamer plus gloves, boots and hood; in summer, a 4/3 steamer is fine

Access
Good road access to all breaks, although long paddle out to The Peak

Other local breaks
Rossnowlagh; Strandhill near Sligo town

While you're there
Take a drive or a hike up into the impressive hills of Yeats Country, named after local poet William Yeats; the views from the summit of 1725 ft Benbulben are spectacular

Ireland is so spoilt for quality surf you could pretty much roll up anywhere on its west coast and have a good chance of catching world-class waves, but as a base Bundoran is hard to beat.

Right in front of the town is 'The Peak', a superb reef break that does just what it says on the tin – peaks up then peels both left and right as a fast, fun wave. The lefts are longer and you'll rarely get it to yourself when it's working, but don't worry. If it's crowded, head north of the town to the lovely beach breaks of Tullan Strand, one of the most consistent beach breaks in Ireland and although popular it'll be easier to get a wave here than at The Peak. People tend to park on the low cliffs above the beach and surf directly beneath them where the wave is more punchy but, if you want a little solitude, just walk along the beach for a few hundred yards to find quieter waves.

Or if you really want to test yourself, take the short drive south of Bundoran to Pampa Point, a shallow, hollow, screaming fast left that has snapped plenty of boards and bodies in the past and will no doubt continue to do so in the future. This is expert-only territory – if you're in any doubt about your skills, give it a miss; there are plenty of other easier options in the area.

Were this all that Bundoran had to offer, you would be a happy surfer, but there's more – there's the 'craic'. The town has a marvellous selection of bars, the best of which is the Bridge Bar. Fantastic breakfasts, Guinness that "slides down the gullet like a penguin in a wetsuit" according to their website, fine live music and you can even check out The Peak from the bar.

So good, so consistent and so varied is the surf around Bundoran that these days the place has become a melting pot of surfers from all over the globe. The Masters World Championships were held here in 2001 and plenty of smaller events have taken place before and since on its shores.

This has good and bad points. On the positive side, you meet some real characters in the surf and the bars. On the negative side, some of these 'real characters' may also be world class surfers so competition for waves can be tough.

But don't let that put you off. When Bundoran is firing you'll get your own great wave at some point and instantly realize why Ireland is the big thing in European cold water surfing these days.

Atlantic
Ocean

Belfast

Mullaghmore

Dublin

Difficulty
Expert only

Hazards
Cold air and water,
especially in winter;
shallow and rocky;
immensely powerful
waves; long and possibly
multi-wave hold downs

Season
Year round but winter
offers the best chance of
monster swells

Water temperature
8 - 16°C (46 – 60°F)

Wetsuit
Full steamer plus gloves,
boots and hood in colder
months; you'll also need
a partner, jet-ski and
buoyancy aid

Access
Good road access to the
headland for viewing;
to surf the break you
need to jet-ski out of
Mullaghmore Harbour

Other local breaks
Bundoran; Strandhill
near Sligo town

While you're there
you'll need a nice relaxing
pint to recover, even
if you've only been
watching the action
from the headland –
head to Sligo town for
a great collection of
bars, restaurants and
nightclubs

MULLAGHMORE, COUNTY SLIGO

Go big – if you dare

County Sligo does not have the best waves on the Emerald Isle but it does have
the biggest. The county is home to exposed Mullaghmore Head, which offers one of the
surfing world's biggest challenges – literally.

The huge waves that pound ashore at Aileens beneath the mighty Cliffs of Moher in
County Clare are more famous, but at the time of writing Mullaghmore Head still boasted
the biggest waves ever ridden in Ireland (if not Europe). A conservative estimate would
put the face of the waves that tow-in partners Gabe Davies and Richie Fitzgerald surfed
in December 2007 at 50 feet.

This is clearly the happy hunting ground of no one other than pro-surfers and nutters
but for the rest of us it's a fantasy that we can indulge in from time to time – that's if you
can imagine what it feels like to drop down the face of a dark grey, wind-lashed beast
that's just risen up out of the Atlantic like something from your worst nightmare.

And if you can't, well, here's what Gabe Davies has to say about it: "Richie and I had actually debated whether or not to go out at all as it was so big, but we'd been waiting for a swell like this for seven years, so in the end the decision was obvious.

"The biggest wave I caught was the biggest wave I've ever surfed anywhere – Hawai'i, Europe, Indonesia, you name it. It was both terrifying and exhilarating at the same time – the drop down the wave face seemed to last forever, and I reckon when I looked up the lip of the wave was maybe 50 feet above me.

"The wave was breaking in front of an exposed rock shelf and the water was a lot shallower than I expected, so if you'd fallen off a big one in the wrong place you'd have been in serious trouble."

By "serious trouble", Gabe means there was every chance of dying.

There are, of course, monster waves elsewhere in the world and all are an incredible challenge to those who take them on, but the combination of cold, shallow water and sea cliffs right in front of the break combined with the raw power of the ocean make Mullaghmore one of the more vicious of this particular breed.

And for those of us who would rather spectate, it's also a great location – you're literally right in front of and above the action. Which is probably as near as most people ever want to get.

North Sea

Newcastle
Upon Tyne

North Yorkshire
Moors

Scarborough

Difficulty
Expert

Hazards
Cold air and water
(especially in winter);
shallow and rocky

Season
Year round but spring–
autumn optimum

Water temperature
4 - 15°C (39 – 59°F)

Wetsuit
Full steamer plus
gloves, boots and hood;
in summer, you may get
away with just a
4/3 steamer

Access
Good road access along
the coast although very
limited or no parking in
villages above the breaks

Other local breaks
Scarborough, Saltburn

While you're there
There's some great hiking
and mountain biking in
the North York Moors
National Park inland, or
take a trip to Whitby
and its Gothic abbey,
said to have been visited
by Dracula

YORKSHIRE REEFS, NORTHERN ENGLAND
Hit the surf in Captain Cook country

There's a hackneyed old phrase in Britain about it being 'grim up north'. Well it's not any longer, at least not if you surf.

But how ironic that the very coastline where Captain James Cook learned the skills that went on to see him 'discover' Hawai'i (and surfing) also has some of the best waves in England – not that the good cap'n would have recognized the quality of the surf.

Indeed, hardly anyone at all recognized the quality of Yorkshire waves until the back end of the 20th century. Whilst south-west England revelled in its self-imposed role as 'surf central' from the 1960s onwards, it wasn't really until the 1980s that the waves of northern England gained any exposure.

Sure, a handful of hardy locals from Yorkshire and Cleveland had been surfing the North Sea since the 1960s, but they were few and far between – and they were made of tough stuff, since wetsuits were not necessarily an essential part of their kit. That takes some doing in water that never gets above about 15°C.

In those early days it was beach breaks such as Saltburn, Scarborough and Cayton Bay that saw all the action, but then some more adventurous locals discovered the area's reef breaks.

Tucked under high, crumbling cliffs that regularly release fossils from their multimillion year imprisonment, flat slabs of kelp covered Jurassic sandstone poke out into the blue–grey waters of the North Sea and trip up swells rolling in from both north and south.

They're invariably set in front of picturesque seaside villages that are thronged with tourists in holiday periods and seriously lacking in parking options unless you're a local, which can mean a bit of a hike to the surf, but it's worth the effort.

Since the prevailing winds in this part of the world are offshore, what the Yorkshire surf pioneers discovered were clean walls of water bursting onto the reefs with remarkable size, power and consistency – all the more remarkable when you consider that the North Sea has a relatively short fetch for all but northerly swells (which generally give the biggest and best surf).

For much of the year, it takes not just skill and experience to surf these waves but commitment too; it's never that warm in Yorkshire and in winter it's useful if you have antifreeze running through your veins rather than blood.

But the cold is soon forgotten when you take the steep drop on an overhead North Sea wall, race the lip and tuck beneath a barrel that may well be the same amber colour as the local beer (coincidentally, also amongst the best in England).

And when you eventually paddle back in and walk through ancient narrow lanes back to your car, you may well be literally following in the footsteps of Captain Cook. Just like in Hawai'i.

River Severn • • Bristol

Atlantic Ocean

Plymouth •

RIVER SEVERN, ENGLAND

Ride up a river on the longest wave of your life

Some would say that the Severn Bore is well named. If like most surfers your idea of good surf is a fast, hollow wave on which to carve your signature, you may indeed find the Bore a bore since it makes but slow and leisurely progress upstream, and only does so a few times a year.

But that's beside the point, for surfing the Severn Bore is all about the experience – and about record breaking, if that's your thing. At the time of writing, the longest ride is more than seven miles.

So, imagine yourself astride your board in the tranquil waters of the River Severn as autumn mists swirl past and, in a Technicolor flash, a kingfisher flits along the riverbank. Gradually, from downriver, a noise like the murmuring of a distant crowd develops into a roar then suddenly a brown wall of water appears across the entire width of the river, topped here and there by a creamy curl where the wave is racing to get ahead of itself.

This is it, the Severn Bore, one of the longest and biggest tidal bores in the world. Catching the wave is pretty easy, and longboarders are at a distinct advantage since the take off is anything but fast and steep. Once you're up and riding you can go for miles, or as long as your legs will take the strain. Or until you collide with another boarder, kayaker or tree branch.

You won't be pulling off much in the way of hot moves, it's more a case of milking the wave for whatever power you can get out of it and trying to ensure you don't lose it, which is why longboards are the best tool for the job. And if you do get left behind there's often a secondary wave following the main one that you can paddle for.

Since the '60s, surfers from all over the world have made their way to the Severn to catch this remarkable wave. It occurs on the biggest tides of the year when Atlantic waters from the Bristol Channel surge up the Severn Estuary as fast as 12 mph and become funnelled between the ever-narrowing river banks to create one of the surfing world's most bizarre spectacles.

If the equinoxes coincide with big Atlantic swells the wave may be as high as six feet, racing upriver, tearing off overhanging tree branches and causing the river bank to collapse here and there. Even so, it's a challenge that any competent surfer can take on, and it's eminently predictable, unlike some waves.

And whatever else it may be, the Severn Bore is definitely not your average wave....

Difficulty
Intermediate – expert

Hazards
Cold water; shallow in places; overhanging branches; other surfers and kayakers (it can get crowded)

Season
Best at equinoxes – go to www.severn-bore.co.uk or www.thelongwave.com for more information

Water temperature
4–16°C (39–61°F)

Wetsuit
Full steamer plus gloves, boots and hood at colder spring equinox (boots also useful for walking to and from river bank)

Access
Good road access along the riverbank although parking can be limited; the areas around Minsterworth, Elmore Back and Hempsted are popular take-off points

Other local breaks
None

While you're there
Head upriver to nearby Gloucester after your surf, for some good pubs and an impressive medieval cathedral

Cardiff

Atlantic
Ocean

Plymouth

Sennen Cove

Difficulty
Beginner – expert

Hazards
Cold air and water in
winter; rips and currents
on bigger swells; rocks at
south end of beach

Season
Year round

Water temperature
7 – 18°C (44 – 64°F)

Wetsuit
Full steamer plus gloves,
boots and hood in
winter; summer
steamer, shortie on
warmer days in summer

Access
By car from
Penzance or St Ives

Other local breaks
St Ives; Praa Sands

While you're there
Head to nearby
Porthcurno where the
water is perhaps even
more turquoise than
Sennen, and there's the
curious open air Minack
Theatre on the cliff top
above the bay

SENNEN COVE,
CORNWALL, ENGLAND

Drive to the end of England for some of the country's best waves

Located at the very south-west tip of England, it's little surprise that Sennen Cove and its neighbouring beach of Gwenver are two of the most consistent beach breaks in the country, so exposed are they to the North Atlantic.

It's not at all unusual for there to be surf here when virtually everywhere else on the south-west coast is flat, and that in itself would be a good enough reason to visit.

But Sennen doesn't just give you a fine selection of peaky beach breaks (which tend to get bigger as you head along the cove towards Gwenver, making it a good spot for surfers of different abilities); it's also one of the loveliest beaches in a county that's full of lovely beaches.

The golden-white sands are speckled with fragments of granite from the local rocks, and the crystals within the rock refract sunlight through the clear Atlantic waters, turning

them a delicious turquoise shade that would be right at home on a tropical shoreline.

You may also spot some serious marine wildlife in these waters, from seals to dolphins, porpoise and basking sharks; the latter can swim into very shallow water, are immense and will frighten the hell out of you if you're out in the surf as they glide past – until you remember that they live off plankton rather than surfers.

The wildness of the coastline – rocks and islets out to sea, the lighthouse of Cape Cornwall in the distance and the knowledge that beyond the bay is nothing but ocean for 3,000 miles – add a touch of the exotic that you don't often find when surfing in England.

It can get busy here in summer but visit out of season and, while you're never likely to get it to yourself, you should have no problem picking off a great wave from time to time. Perhaps the only downside to surfing here is that it takes a little bit of effort to access the better waves. It's either a long walk up the beach from the car park or an easier trot down hundreds of steps from above the beach, which can seem like a mountain climb when you have to retrace your steps at the end of a long session.

But you can take solace in the knowledge that when your session is over you can fuel up at the cool beach café or the old whitewashed pub in the village just across from the lifeboat station.

Add all of this together and you get an eclectic mix of traditional and modern that are well worth driving to the end of England for.

North
Sea

Swansea
Pembroke London
Plymouth

Difficulty
Beginner – expert

Hazards
Cold air and water in
winter; some breaks
shallow and rocky;
currents

Season
Year round

Water temperature
7 – 18°C (44 – 64°F)

Wetsuit
Full steamer, plus
gloves, boots and hood
in winter; shortie
possible in summer

Access
By car from
Pembroke or Tenby

Other local breaks
Broadhaven South;
Manorbier

While you're there
If you're into castles,
check out the splendid
eleventh century
examples at nearby
Pembroke, Carew and
Manorbier

FRESHWATER WEST, PEMBROKESHIRE, WALES

Ride the waves where the latter day Robin Hood strutted his stuff

Let's just assume you've hit it right and arrived at 'Fresh West' on a late summer day when the sun is shining bright and warm, a gentle offshore breeze flits through the dunes and out to sea, and a clean, head high swell rolls ashore.

Paddle out, watch side on as the green-blue, peaky beach breaks throw out a glistening little barrel and spill their power onto the golden sand and, unlikely as it seems, you might just think you're in south-west France. Yes, the surf at Freshwater West is, on its day, comparable with pretty much anywhere else in Europe.

Those days don't occur too often, of course, which is what makes the place so special. Even so, most Welsh surfers would readily regard 'Fresh' as the country's best beach break, and it's also a pretty cool place to hang out for a few days too – any summer

weekend when there's a good swell running will see a rash of campervans parked up above the beach.

Located in Britain's only coastal national park, the mile-long golden sands are hemmed in by low cliffs at either end and backed by high dunes that offer ideal shelter for sunbathing and picnicking after your session. There's a bit of a fly in the ointment in the form of the nearby oil refinery and power stations in adjacent Milford Haven Estuary – although you're more likely to smell these than see them – and there's the occasional 'bang!' of the military playing soldiers at Castlemartin Range behind the beach. (Perhaps only in the UK could such developments take place right next to, or even in, a national park.)

Nowhere is perfect, but Freshwater West is probably as good a chance as you have in Wales of finding near perfect waves. What's more, it's big enough to handle the increasing numbers of surfers who visit from all over Wales on a good swell, it works at most stages of the tide, there are peaks along the length of the bay and even a couple of other serious surf spots close by that the curious/intrepid may discover with a bit of initiative.

If you still find it hard to believe that there's good surf in Wales, consider the fact that surf contests – including the Europeans – have been held at Freshwater West since the 1970s, which is as good an indication as any of the place's quality and consistency.

In fact, the swell even gave 'Robin Hood' a hard time recently; the big battle scene in the blockbuster film starring Russell Crowe was shot here, with occasional interruptions as a summer swell tossed boats and Hollywood stars hither and thither.

Difficulty
Beginner–expert

Hazards
Rocks around the point;
rips on bigger swells

Season
Year round

Water temperature
8–18°C (46–64°F)

Wetsuit
Full steamer plus gloves,
boots and hood in winter;
4/3 steamer, maybe
shortie in midsummer

Access
Good road access
to the beach

Other local breaks
Tronoën; Porzcarn

While you're there
You could have a go at
kiteboarding – lessons
and hire available
at the beach

LA TORCHE, BRITTANY

La Torche shines bright on France's Celtic coastline

La Torche is possibly the most popular break in Brittany, and there's a reason for that: it's good; it's pretty consistent; it has a variety of breaks including Pors Carn, which works on the prevailing south-westerly winds; and it's also a really nice beach irrespective of the surf.

But there's more to La Torche than all of the above. This is just one of many good breaks in Brittany, and you may well come here strictly for the surf but you'll probably leave having been seduced by the unique mix of culture and landscape that make up this most Celtic corner of France.

The links with the other Celtic surfing nations of Europe are palpable. Not only does Brittany have its own language (Breton, which has very obvious connections with Cornish in particular but also with Irish, Welsh and Gaelic), it also has land- and seascapes that have a very Celtic feel about them.

With its exposed, rocky and convoluted coastline (which means there's always a reasonable chance of finding offshore conditions somewhere), hidden green valleys, mist shrouded uplands and sturdily built harbours, towns and villages designed to withstand the howling wind and rain that regularly sweep in from the sea, it will be familiar to surfers from all the Celtic regions, so much so that sometimes it's easy to forget just which country you're in when you're sitting on your board and gazing shorewards.

But La Torche and Brittany do have one slight advantage over their counterparts to the north: year round, it's a degree or two warmer in this part of the world, which can mean the difference between chilly and frigid in winter and full suit or shortie in summer.

When La Torche is at its best, say in late summer, sun beaming from a cloudless sky and a clean, hurricane swell thumping into the beach, it's comparable with anywhere in France. There's a right hand point break that can get as much size as most people are ever likely to want, while the banks on the beach can be punchy and fast – hollow, even – and provide great fun rides that are often quite long too.

It'll be busy in these conditions, and you may also have windsurfers and kiteboarders clogging things up if there's a bit of a breeze, but if the crowds get too much there are plenty of other breaks in the region and a little exploration may well bring rewards.

For many surfers, a thorough exploration of Brittany will provide all the waves you'll require of a surf trip. For others, it makes a great and conveniently short detour on the drive down to the more popular, warmer waves of south-west France.

Either way, La Torche is well worth including in your itinerary for an essential taste of Breton surfing.

Difficulty
Intermediate – expert

Hazards
Shallow water;
overhanging branches

Season
Year round but winter
may be very cold

Water temperature
2–19°C (35–66°F)

Wetsuit
Full steamer plus gloves,
boots and hood in colder
months; boardshorts in
midsummer

Access
Flights to Munich; public
transport to city centre

Other local breaks
River Reuss, Bremgarten,
Switzerland

While you're there
Pop into the city's beer
halls, including the
famous Hofbräuhaus am
Platzl, for a few cold ones

MUNICH, GERMANY

Wetsuits among the city suits: river surfing on Munich's standing wave

There are plenty of rivers that hold surfable standing waves, but none is as well known as Munich's River Eisbach (which translates as 'Ice Brook' – there's a clue there as to what the water temperature is like).

Apparently, this tributary of the River Isar was first surfed as long ago as 1972, although it's only in recent years that the landlocked surfers of Bavaria have regularly ridden the standing wave that is produced as the river bursts out from an underground tunnel at Haus der Kunst in the middle of the city. Indeed, there's an annual surf contest on the river, despite the fact that, in theory at least, surfing here is technically verboten as far as the authorities are concerned.

The Isar has probably become the world's most famous surfable river wave thanks to its location in the middle of Munich, which means it is easily accessible as well as being a good stage for the exhibitionists and poseurs who invariably make up an unhealthy percentage of any local surfing population. Whatever the reason, whenever there's a good 'swell' running – which in this case means a good flow of water – the waist high wave will invariably have someone riding it.

This being Germany, things are done in an orderly fashion, one at a time. The wave is only big enough to hold one surfer so Munich's surf dudes queue along the river bank while their buddies take their turn, watched by bemused onlookers from a bridge overlooking the 'break'.

Depending on the skill of the surfer the ride may last a few seconds or a few minutes, with standard manoeuvres consisting of cutbacks, off-the-tops (not that there's much of a top to go off), 360s and the like, and it's even possible to buy locally manufactured boards that are specifically designed for this wave (a 5' 11" Buster, since you ask).

Surfing the Isar looks deceptively easy and most competent surfers will indeed find it straightforward enough after a little practice. The water is shallow, however, so wipeouts can hurt, there's the prospect of bashing into the river bank to consider and, when you do eventually tire or wipeout, the rapid flow of the river will pop you out the back of the wave and carry you some distance downstream before you've gathered your wits and clambered back onto your board to paddle to the bank.

There's a certain amount of localism here and fools may not be suffered too gladly. Fortunately, the city also has another river wave for less confident surfers a little further upriver, the Flosslande in Thalkirchen, which is smaller and has a less powerful flow.

Munich isn't likely to be high on most surfers' list of destinations. But hey, it's a cool city with a fine beer festival every October, and if you're paying a flying visit or passing through en route to a more regular surf destination, why not take your board and ride the urban wave?

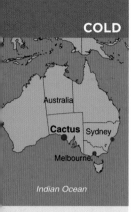

Australia

Cactus Sydney

Melbourne

Indian Ocean

Difficulty
Expert

Hazards
Cold water, hot sun, lack of drinking water; powerful waves; shallow water; sharp reefs; sharks; snakes; flies; remote; limited accommodation and camping options

Season
Year round

Water temperature
12–14°C (53–57°F)

Wetsuit
4/3 or 3/2 steamer, boots

Access
Most breaks accessible by dirt roads but a long drive from 'civilization'

Other local breaks
Witzig's (named after the famous '60s surf movie maker) to the south; Crushers and Supertubes to the north

While you're there
This is the ideal place to chill out with some fishing or a good book and a cold beer, as there's not much else to do...

CACTUS, SOUTH AUSTRALIA

Like the plant it's named after, Cactus is sharp and to the point

Fringed by the hot, dusty, red Nullarbor Plain inland and one of the world's wildest stretches of oceans to seaward, Cactus sits at the eastern end of the Great Australian Bight. And when you consider what lives in the shimmering green waters of this corner of the Southern Ocean, you could be forgiven for thinking the cartographers spelled the name incorrectly.

For the deep waters off Cactus are a shark breeding ground – bronze whalers and great whites in particular seem to favour this spot and have been known to take chunks out of surfers on several occasions over the 40-odd years that this area has been surfed.

If that wasn't enough, back on shore there are poisonous snakes, spiky plants and exasperating clouds of flies to deal with, along with hardcore locals who may not be as mean as the wildlife but probably won't go out of their way to make you feel at home.

For many visitors it can seem a pretty harsh and demanding environment, whether onshore or offshore, so you really have got to want to surf here to make the long drive from Adelaide or the two to three day trek from Perth in the far west.

However, if fast, shallow, barrelling reef breaks are your thing, Cactus and the breaks around it may just tempt you. The small peninsula where Cactus is located juts out into the eastern end of the Great Australian Bight and its west coast picks up tons of swell emanating from low pressure systems barrelling endlessly around the Roaring Forties to the south although, ironically, Cactus is not generally the best break in the area.

When it's on, however, it's a speedy, hollow left that's one of the easier breaks in the area to deal with, making it a good introduction to surfing hereabouts. If this isn't challenging enough for you, wait for a bigger day and try Castles, another left hander that rips across the reef at high speed and will nail you if you don't move fast.

You can ratchet the fear factor up a few more notches by surfing Outside Castles; not only is this even more powerful and just as fast as the inside wave, it breaks in front of a deep water channel where the men in grey suits like to hang out, and this is where most of the area's shark attacks have occurred.

For most people this is probably pushing it a bit more than is strictly necessary, so you'll be glad to know there are several other breaks in the area that don't harbour quite so much multi-toothed submarine wildlife, but none are especially easy waves to ride.

But then this is Cactus – it's not meant to be easy.

Melbourne

Indian
Ocean

Hobart

Shipsterns Bluff

Difficulty
Expert only

Hazards
Cold water; strong rips
and currents; shallow;
rocky; remote; sharks

Season
Year round

Water temperature
11 – 15°C (51 – 59°F)

Wetsuit
Winter steamer and
boots; possibly hood in
colder months

Access
Difficult

Other local breaks
There are great waves all
along Tasmania's south-
east coast

While you're there
If you're visiting in
summer, check out
the Hobart Summer
Festival, which coincides
with the finish of the
Sydney-Hobart Yacht Race
in late December

SHIPSTERNS BLUFF, TASMANIA

A devil of a wave on Tasmania's southern shore

Sydney's *Daily Telegraph* newspaper once ran a feature on Shipsterns Bluff under the heading "Places to Surf Before You Die" but this hideous mutant of a break could just as easily be described as a place to surf where you may die.

'Shippies' is as unrepresentative of Tasmanian surfing (which in this area consists largely of excellent south-east coast point and beach breaks) as is Mullaghmore Head of Irish surfing, but it's definitely a place all surfers will want to visit, even if only to watch the wave break.

The island has always been a little off the radar as far as Australian surfing is concerned, despite records of people having surfed here since the 1920s. Perhaps this is because of its relative isolation and relatively cold water, but with the 'discovery' of Shipsterns Bluff, that situation has changed somewhat.

First surfed as recently as 1997 by Tassie surfer Andy Campbell, the Bluff is one of the world's heaviest waves, powered by thumping Roaring Forties swells that throw themselves ashore on the island's south-eastern shores, forming a stepped wall of water that snarls and roars as it blasts all its energy into a few hundred metres of shallow reef.

Overshadowed by the vertiginous cliffs from which the wave gets its name (it was once known as Devil's Point, which is perhaps more appropriate), the long but lovely two-hour walk into Shipsterns Bluff and the intimidating nature of both the shoreline and the wave ensure that, while it can be relatively busy in the water on a good swell, it's not likely to become overcrowded.

If it's too challenging for you – and there's no shame in that, very few recreational surfers will want to take on such a beast – you can enjoy grandstand viewing of the action only a hundred metres or so from the break and watch as those who do dare to take it on freefall down the face, negotiate the various lips and steps as the face doubles in size, and then hang on for grim death as they hurtle towards safety on the wave's shoulder.

Those who make it may get barrelled; those who don't will get the beating of their lives as tons of dark, glassy Southern Ocean swell hammers them into the shallow reef below.

Andy Campbell described how his legs "felt weak from apprehension and fear" on the occasion when he pioneered surfing here, and it takes absolutely no imagination at all to empathise with him on that.

But as he also points out, if you dare to take on the wave and pull it off, it can change your entire focus and attitude to surfing. As to whether it's worth the risk – well, only you can decide that...

Auckland
Raglan

Tasman
Sea

Christchurch

Difficulty
Intermediate – expert

Hazards
Rocky bottom; rips on
bigger swells

Season
Year round

Water temperature
13 - 18°C (55 – 64°F)

Wetsuit
Full steamer (4/3 or 3/2)
plus boots in winter

Access
Good road access
to the beach

Other local breaks
Indicators; Whale Bay

While you're there
Raglan has a great live
music scene, including
regular open mic nights at
the Town Hall and the Old
School Arts Centre

RAGLAN, NORTH ISLAND, NEW ZEALAND

Surf the endless walls discovered by the Endless Summer crew

Within the Kiwi surfing world, Raglan's Manu Bay is beyond famous. Whether that's a good or bad thing is open to question, but since it's generally regarded as one of the finest left-hand point breaks in the world, it's hardly surprising that virtually every surf traveller who visits New Zealand finds themselves drawn here.

Some eight kilometres from the laid back town of Raglan, Manu Bay first gained exposure in the classic 1960s surf movie Endless Summer, since when there's been an endless procession of surfers paddling out to ride for hundreds of yards along its perfectly lined up walls.

What's more, this is not an especially ferocious wave – at least not when it's a modest size – which means less skilled surfers can have a go at taking it on. Together with easy access, this means that it is normal for there to be crowds, and a certain amount of localism may be encountered by those who push their luck. Which doesn't sound too inviting.

But the thing about Manu Bay is that you'll invariably end up setting aside any perfectly understandable dislike of crowds when you see a clean swell wrap around the point and peel machine-like for up to 300 yards into the bay.

Add to that the mellow surf-oriented vibe of the area and you'll find it hard to resist the urge to paddle out and at least have a go at catching one of those busy waves.

And when you do? Well, take the drop and turn left and that wall just seems to feather for ever in front of you, throwing forward into the occasionally barrel, until you have to think about kicking out because your legs are actually beginning to ache – and that's when you realize it's all very definitely worth the effort.

For hardcore surfers, the best time to visit is winter, when powerful swells emanating from the Roaring Forties roll ashore with agreeable consistency and, although chilly and relatively unpredictable, the climate isn't by any means unbearable. This also gives you the option of taking in some of the ski and snowboard action at Mount Taranaki or Mount Ruapahu. Like many of the waves in New Zealand, things tend to be a little more laid back on the country's ski slopes than those of Europe or North America, as well as pretty good value.

Irrespective of when you visit New Zealand, the Raglan area has got to be worth a stop over. And when you've had your fill here, there are countless less crowded spots to be discovered on the North Island.

Tasman
Sea

Auckland

Mahia
Peninsula

Wellington

Difficulty
Beginner – expert

Hazards
Cold in winter; some
breaks quite remote;
rips and currents

Season
Year round

Water temperature
11 - 19°C (51 – 66°F)

Wetsuit
Full steamer and boots
in winter; 3/2 steamer,
perhaps shortie in
summer

Access
Varies, although most
popular breaks can be
accessed by road

Other local breaks
Last Chance to the north
of the peninsula; Black's
Beach to the west

While you're there
There are some good
hiking trails around the
peninsula

MAHIA PENINSULA, NORTH ISLAND, NEW ZEALAND

Take your pick – there are waves for everyone on the wild Mahia Peninsula

The Mahia Peninsula makes a fine alternative – or addition – to a surf trip to New Zealand's legendary Raglan. Located on the North Island's east coast and thrusting like a Stone Age dagger into the Pacific Ocean, this wild, undeveloped and mountainous peninsula picks up pretty consistent swell all year round.

It's less than a day's drive from the busier west coast and, although it doesn't receive quite as much swell, the Mahia Peninsula makes up for this by having consistent south-westerly winds, which are offshore at many of the best breaks. Should the wind switch direction, all is not lost since the peninsula has shorelines facing almost every point of the compass, which means there's always a good chance of encountering offshore conditions.

It's also somewhat drier than the west coast here – always a good thing when you're squeezing in and out of a wetsuit – and while there's an even more laid back vibe than there is around Raglan the locals are understandably protective of their breaks, so a mellow approach is always appreciated, especially amongst the native Maori population.

There are plenty of opportunities to 'discover' your own break in an area that has relatively few points of easy access to the coast but, unless you're dead set on exploring, you'll find plenty to go around with the tried and tested breaks on the peninsula.

The small settlement of Opoutama is a good first port of call, since it has an extremely consistent south-westerly facing beach break that makes a good introduction to the area. The blue-green waters are rarely still here at a latitude that is equivalent to that of northern Portugal, with air and water temperatures quite similar, although if the region's predominant south-westerly winds are blowing you'll need to pop across the narrow isthmus to the north, where you can check out the inviting reefs at Te Kapu or the popular left-hander at Mahia Spit.

North and south of these breaks are a selection of beach and point breaks to suit everyone from frantic groms to mellow longboarders, with the somewhat remote and consequently quiet Diner's Beach perhaps the most consistent spot around.

Mahia has about it a feel that harks back to earlier, less commercialized times in places such as Cornwall and South Wales. There aren't surf shops on every corner, people are still happy to pass the time of day both in and out of the water and you can see where New Zealand gets its reputation for being a little behind the times – in the most positive of ways.

Paraguay

Chile

Quintero

Uruguay

Argentina

South Atlantic
Ocean

Difficulty
Intermediate – expert

Hazards
Cold water; strong
rips and currents on
big swells; some
remote breaks

Season
Year round

Water temperature
12 – 17°C (53 – 62°F)

Wetsuit
Winter steamer and
boots; 4/3 or 3/2 steamer
in summer

Access
Fly into Santiago and rent
a car for relatively easy
access to main breaks

Other local breaks
There are world class
waves along pretty
much the entire length
of Chile's coast

While you're there
It's worth taking time
out for a trip to the
Andes – go hiking
in summer, skiing or
boarding in winter

CENTRAL CHILE

There's a distinct leaning to the left in this part of the world

The area between the small coastal village of Pichilemu in the south of Chile and Quintero in the north is one of the most blessed on the planet as far as surf is concerned. Flat days are a rarity (you're more likely to end up searching for somewhere small enough rather than big enough) and for goofies in particular this is surf heaven, with one long left after another barrelling shorewards year round.

Nothing is perfect, though, and to offset all this surf munificence you'll have to deal with relatively cold water all year, increasing crowds as surfing quite understandably takes off more and more in Chile, and difficult access to some spots, although the latter is only a minor problem given the wealth of waves available in this part of the country.

The secret of the phenomenal number of world class point breaks around halfway along Chile's ridiculously long 2672 miles of coastline (the country is 25 times longer than it is wide) lies in the continual pulses of swells generated from lows to the south, particularly in the Antarctic and Roaring Forties region. These roll north and, with a submarine trench of up to 8,000 m deep just offshore, have nothing to bar their progress until they hit the Chilean coastline.

In this region, this just happens to consist of a series of north and north-west facing bays into which the swell wraps to produce the region's delightful left handers; add to that predominantly south to south-west (i.e. offshore) winds outside the winter months and it really would seem that when God created Chile he had surfers (and wetsuit manufacturers) in mind.

There are various beach and reef breaks throughout the area, too, and on smaller swells these should be investigated for their fun peaks and barrels, although they'll often be busy, especially in summer, since the capital Santiago is relatively close.

But you don't come to Chile to surf waist high beach breaks. A good option, if you like to save the best 'til last, is to rent a car in Santiago and drive north along the Panamerican Highway for around 62 miles before heading toward Quintero on the coast.

This area is where surfing began in Chile in the 1970s, and it's consequently one of the more popular surf zones with a mix of points, river mouths, reefs and beach breaks, but as you head south past Valparaiso and the long lefts at spots such as Algarobbo, La Boquilla and Matanzas, you'll hit on the long lefts for which the region is so famous, all the way down to Pichilemu.

And note that these are only the readily accessible breaks. For example, there are large swathes of coastline in between Pichilemu and Matanzas with limited or no road access, where who knows what you may find if you feel inclined to explore – although it's a good bet it'll be more of the same.

South Atlantic
Ocean

Argentina

Chile

Falkland Islands

Difficulty
Intermediate – expert

Hazards
Cold; remote; orcas;
sea lions; powerful
swells; rocks; currents;
unexploded land mines

Season
Year round in theory,
although winter too
harsh for most

Water temperature
2–12°C (35–54°F)

Wetsuit
Winter steamer, boots,
gloves and hood
for most of the year

Access
Difficult

Other local breaks
There are waves in
Bahia Grande on
mainland Argentina and
also along the eastern
coast of Tierra del Fuego

While you're there
Try wildlife watching
when the weather is
good; book reading
when it's bad

FALKLAND ISLANDS

Wild waters and wild weather –
so don't forget your comb

Located at a latitude of around 52° S off the eastern tip of South America, this
British dependency is surrounded by the cold, storm lashed South Atlantic and receives
a mighty amount of swell year round, particularly on its south–east coast, which is
convenient since this is where the capital city Stanley is located.

However, unless you live on the islands or get sent there as part of your UK military
service, you really do need to be very eager to get totally away from it all to surf the
Falkland Islands.

It's obviously costly to get here and, apart from a few known spots surfed by military
personnel, you'll have to venture along wild coastlines thrashed by even wilder waters and
inhabited by serious wildlife along the lines of killer whales and sea lions (the penguins
are a little less serious). Things are made that bit more hazardous by the unexploded and
unmapped ordnance left behind as a legacy of the Falkland's War in the 1980s.

You encounter the most regularly surfed breaks almost as soon as you arrive on the archipelago, with the uninspiringly named Surf Bay on the airport road regularly producing heavy, fast beach breaks, whilst Bertha's Beach at Mare Bay has perhaps an even better wave. The proximity of military facilities to the island's capital is the reason these are the prime surf spots, with service personnel enjoying far quieter waves here than they ever would back in the UK, and you could easily make do with just these two spots as they'll never be crowded and are very consistent.

If you want to explore, however, a brief glimpse at a map will reveal a convoluted coastline of bays, points and headlands facing every direction of the compass, which means the wind will always be offshore somewhere – albeit howling offshore a lot of the time.

Combine this with consistent swell and you can see that the potential for surf discoveries is high. And the islands also have 250 miles of road criss-crossing them, so you can access more territory than you might expect. This territory is a mix of windblown moorland fringed by steel blue seas, populated by 700,000 sheep (compared to just over 3,000 humans) and rarely warm enough for anything other than several layers of clothing and an appropriately thick layer of neoprene when you're out in the waves.

But catch the Falklands on a day when the sun shines and the wind drops to a mere breeze and flicks the top off glittering waves, and you may just have stumbled across a cold water surf paradise, even if only until the next storm comes racing past.

Difficulty
Expert

Hazards
Cold; remote; orcas; sea
lions; rocks; currents;
collapsing icebergs

Season
Summer only

Water temperature
Minus 2–2°C (28–36°F);
the sea can actually
remain liquid when its
temperature dips below
freezing, thanks to its
salt content

Wetsuit
7mm steamer or drysuit,
boots, gloves and hood

Access
Extremely difficult

Other local breaks
Rugged Island and
Lowe Island also have
surfable waves

While you're there
Enjoy some of the world's
most amazing wildlife
watching and landscapes

ANTARCTIC ICEBERG

Surfing at the end of the world

With increasing numbers of cruise ships taking tourists to the icy blue shores of
Antarctica, you could in theory take a board on one of these costly cruises and surf here.
But the reality is that access to any breaks you may stumble across will be restricted in
order to protect the natural environment and, being realistic, a side trip to go surfing is
never really going to happen.

Which means the only other option is to organize your own boat surfari to the end of
the world. And having the advantage of a boat to live on and surf from means that you
can surf what is possibly the most bizarre 'point break' ever – one that is breaking off an
open ocean iceberg.

This is what Dr Mark Renneker, Edwin Salem, Chris Malloy and an assorted crew of
Californian surfers encountered on the first ever surf trip south of the Antarctic Circle.
While it's a fair bet that the particular break they discovered will never be surfed again,
since it will have since melted away, there are plenty of other icebergs down there that
may produce the goods. But get there fast – apparently they're an endangered species.

Renneker and co. discovered their icy waves whilst sailing south towards Deception
Island in search of more traditional breaks, through an area of the South Atlantic

littered with thousands of icebergs of all sizes. In crisp, clear skies of deepest blue and sailing through an azure sea where the wind rippled the swell into emerald lines, they unexpectedly came across a shoulder high peak peeling left and right from a submerged ice platform onto a small 'beach' on the 'berg.

Kitting up to surf the wave took some time, dry suits being the protection of choice, after which Salem and Malloy leapt over the rail into waters that were only just above freezing, paddled to the peak and coolly (in every sense of the word) took wave after wave – the most southerly surfers in the world.

Each ride would end in the shallow waters of the 'beach', where the task of walking out to paddling depth was anything but simple. Slip-sliding on the planet's most friction free natural material, it took more balance to wade back out across wave-slicked ice into water deep enough for paddling than it did to ride the waves.

This was undoubtedly the most unusual wave of the trip – perhaps one of the most unusual waves ever surfed – but the guys chanced across more traditional breaks, too, such as point breaks on Nelson Island and Deception Island.

There is a limit to how far south any surfari can take you, of course, since eventually you reach a place where sea is frozen. And very few surfers are ever likely to have the chance to surf the forever empty peaks of Antarctica.

But it's nice to know that there are surfable waves in this almost forgotten corner of the world, and it goes to show just how much surf there is on the planet.

6	Mentawai Islands, Indonesia	© ImageState/Alamy
8	One Palm Point, Western Java, Indonesia	© Buzz Pictures/Alamy
10	Sumbawa, Indonesia	© JS Callahan/tropicalpix
12	Desert Point, Lombok, Indonesia	© Paul Kennedy/Surfpix
14	Siargao, Philippines	© JS Callahan/tropicalpix
16	Papua New Guinea	© JS Callahan/tropicalpix
18	Andaman Island	© JS Callahan/tropicalpix
20	Sri Lanka	© JS Callahan/tropicalpix
22	The Maldives	© Alf Alderson/Surfpix
24	Bay of Bengal	© JS Callahan / tropicalpix
26	Tongatapu, Tonga	© Sean Davey/Surfpix
28	Viti Levu, Fiji	© Sean Davey/Surfpix
30	Tahiti	© Sean Davey/Surfpix
32	New Caledonia	© JS Callahan/tropicalpix
34	Solomon Islands	© WaterFrame/Alamy
36	Rarotonga, Cook Islands	© Sean Davey/Surfpix
38	Savai'i and Upolu, Western Samoa	© Sean Davey/Surfpix
40	Micronesia	© Sean Davey/Surfpix
42	Northern New South Wales/Southern Queensland, Australia	© Sean Davey/Surfpix
44	Taiwan	© JS Callahan/tropicalpix
46	China	© JS Callahan/tropicalpix
48	Oman and Dubai	© JS Callahan/tropicalpix
50	Comoros Islands	© JS Callahan/tropicalpix
52	Madagascar	© JS Callahan/tropicalpix
54	Réunion Island	© JS Callahan/tropicalpix
56	Durban, South Africa	© JS Callahan/tropicalpix
58	Dakar, Senegal	© JS Callahan/tropicalpix/Alamy
60	Ghana	© JS Callahan/tropicalpix
62	Liberia	© JS Callahan/tropicalpix
64	São Tomé	© JS Callahan/tropicalpix
66	Cape Verde Islands	© imagebroker/Alamy
68	Great Abaco and Eleuthera, Bahamas	© Chris Clinton/Getty Images
70	Barbados	© Tony Arruza/Alamy
72	Costa Rica, Caribbean Coast	© JS Callahan/tropicalpix
74	Costa Rica, Pacific Coast	© Jamie Bott/Surfpix
76	Panama	© JS Callahan/tropicalpix
78	El Salvador	© Scott Aichner/Surfpix
80	Puerto Escondido, Mexico	© Scott Aichner/Surfpix
82	Colima & NW Michoacan, Mexico	© Buzz Pictures/Alamy
84	Baja Peninsula, Mexico	© Mark A. Johnson/Alamy
86	Oahu, North shore, Hawai'i	© Scott Aichner/Surfpix
88	Maui, Hawai'i	© Sean Davey/Surfpix
90	Hossegor and Les Landes, France	© Jeff Flindt/Surfpix
92	Mundaka, Northern Spain	© Jeff Flindt/Surfpix
94	Ericeira, Portugal	© Jeff Flindt, Photos registered at the Library of Congress
96	Southern Portugal	© Jeff Flindt/Surfpix
98	North West Italy	© francesco survara/Alamy
100	Sardinia, Italy	© Jeff Flindt
102	Madeira Island	© imagebroker/Alamy
104	Lanzarote, Canary Islands	© Jeff Flindt, Photos registered at the Library of Congress